# How to Live & Work

**In this Series**

# LIVE & WORK
# IN FRANCE

**A handbook for short and long stay visitors**

Nicole Prevost Logan

Second Edition

**How To Books**

**British Library Cataloguing in Publication Data**
A catalogue record for this book is available from the British Library.

© Copyright 1990 and 1993 by Intercultural Press. First published in 1990.
Second edition published in 1993 by How To Books Ltd, Plymbridge House,
Estover Road, Plymouth PL6 7PZ, United Kingdom. Tel: (0752) 735251/
695745. Fax: (0752) 695699. Telex: 45635.

*Note*: The material contained in this book is set out in good faith for general
guidance and no liability can be accepted for loss or expense incurred as a
result of relying in particular circumstances on statements made in the book.
The laws and regulations are complex and liable to change, and readers
should check the current position with the relevant authorities before making
personal arrangements.

Typeset by PDQ Typesetting, Stoke-on-Trent
Printed and bound by the Cromwell Press, Broughton Gifford, Melksham

# Contents

**List of Maps**

Regions

Nord

Picardie

Haute-Normandie

Basse-Normandie

Ile de France

Champagne

Lorraine

Alsace

Bretagne

Pays de la Loire

Centre

Bourgogne

Franche-Comté

Poitou-Charentes

Limousin

Auvergne

Rhône-Alpes

Bastia

Corsica

Aquitaine

Midi-Pyrénées

Languedoc Roussillon

Provence-Alpes Côte d'Azur

# 1
# Introduction
# to France

## OVERVIEW: THE GEOGRAPHY OF FRANCE

France is the largest country in western Europe, yet only 650 miles separate the Belgian border in the north from the Mediterranean, or the city of Strasbourg on the Rhine River from the western tip of Brittany.

The terrain and scenery of France vary widely. There are snow-capped mountains in the Alps, a popular area for winter sports; lush plains with cultivated fields and market gardens around Paris; sunny, rocky tourist beaches in the Côte d'Azur; rugged, dour mountains in the Pyrenees; rain- and windswept holiday resorts in the northwest; flat sandy forests in the Landes and wild moorland in the Cevennes.

In general the south and the southeast of France are mountainous; the north and west are low. The hills and plateaux of the Massif Central, with its extinct volcanoes, hot springs and many rivers, occupy the middle part of France.

France has modern cities and medieval villages; vineyards and miles of poplar-lined country lanes; a bleak black country in the industrial north; and the pure light of Provence, so dear to the French impressionists, in the south.

France's climate is kept temperate by the Gulf Stream. In the low plains of the north, the west and around Paris, the Atlantic Ocean influences the weather, bringing rain, fog and grey skies. Winters are mild, summers cool; temperatures range from the mid-forties to the mid-seventies. A more continental climate prevails in the eastern and central parts of France, with cold winters and heavy snow at times, and clearly differentiated seasons. On the Mediterranean coast there are occasional cold winters, but the weather is usually dry and sunny, with the lowest temperatures in the fifties. Summers are hot and the vegetation is almost subtropical.

**Departments and Major Cities**

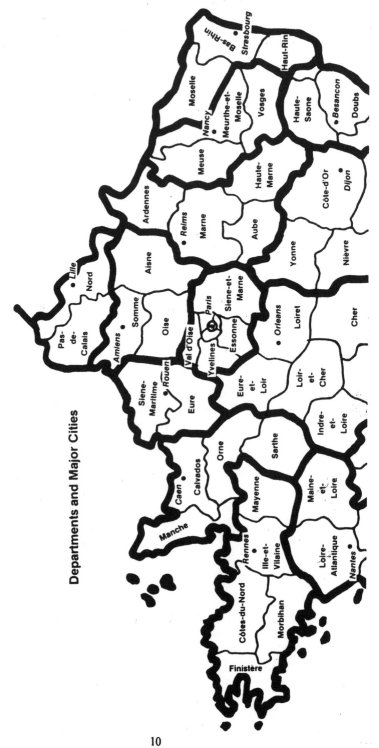

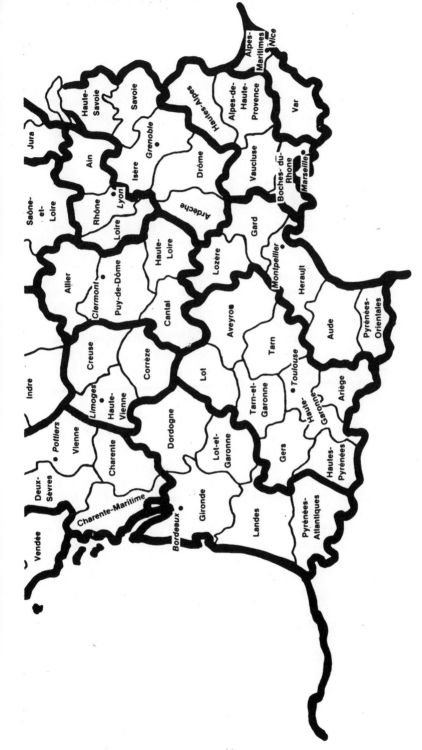

11

France has a superb network of rivers and canals, which constitutes 40 per cent of all the waterways of Europe. The five main rivers are the Seine, the Rhine, the Loire, the Rhône and the Garonne. Work is underway to connect the Rhine and the Rhône by a 140-mile canal with 24 locks; this will make Paris virtually an inland port.

## THE PEOPLE OF FRANCE

### A few statistics

The total population of France is around 56 million, with an average density of 250 people per square mile (the UK, Germany, Italy, the Netherlands and Belgium all have a much higher population density). More than 70 per cent of the French people live in the urban industrial areas of the north, the east and the Rhône Valley, while some mountainous out-of-the-way areas are, by contrast, almost deserted.

Paris is by far France's largest city, with 2,200,000 inhabitants. The greater Paris region has a population of ten million. Lyon and Marseille regions follow with more than one million each, then Lille, Bordeaux and Toulouse.

### Origins

Originally of Nordic, Alpine and Mediterranean stock, the French have experienced several waves of immigration. Between the two world wars, nearly three million immigrants, mostly of Slavic origin, came to France. In recent years great numbers have come from North Africa, particularly French expatriates (or **pieds noirs**— literally 'black feet') and Algerian refugees. Over four million foreigners live in France, roughly 8 per cent of the total population. The largest number are Portuguese, followed by Algerians, Italians, Spaniards, Moroccans, Tunisians, Yugoslavs and Poles. In all, 122 nationalities are represented, and there is a thriving English expatriate community in every major city.

### Immigration policies

Traditionally, France has had an open door policy towards immigrants, but the recent influx has forced the government to reverse its policy. In recent years more stringent requirements have been established for entry into France. The law strictly limits immigration and encourages immigrant workers to return to their country of origin.

However, immigration should present considerably fewer problems for those coming from other member countries of the European Community. Now that the Single Market has arrived, holders of a full UK passport, for example, should find less and less red tape in their way. The major sticking point of the new immigration laws is that it is now more important than ever to have the proper documentation ready *before* entering the country.

## Declining birthrate

France's declining birthrate troubles the Government. It has dropped below the 2.1 per cent deemed necessary to demographers to maintain the population at its present level. To encourage population growth, the Government grants tax deductions and offers special allowances and benefits, such as reduced fares on trains, to large families. Even unmarried mothers receive comfortable allowances.

Fourteen per cent of the population is over 65 years of age. The large numbers of elderly people are a heavy burden for the working population, who must contribute to their pensions.

## A society in transition

Two main themes dominate contemporary French life. One is France's shift to an urban, industrialised society. This is true not only of Paris but also of many other cities which, until World War II, were relatively sleepy provincial centres. Many are now experiencing the bustle, noise, housing problems and traffic jams found in any large metropolitan area.

The other theme is the considerable shift of population from the cities to the suburbs. The suburban growth is immediately noticeable to travellers as they drive from the airport into Paris. The growth around Paris in recent years is so dramatic that it can be described as practically explosive—commercial, industrial and administrative centres are increasingly moving to the suburbs.

There is also a shift from large urban centres to attractive, formerly sparsely populated areas. A recent 'migration' from the industrial north to the more thinly populated south has occurred with the encouragement of the Government; today sunny Provence is one of France's booming regions.

Although small shopkeepers, artisans, and family enterprises still exist (in fact, most employment in France today is provided by companies employing fewer than 50 people), the increasing number of large corporations, many of them state-owned, and the acceleration of advanced technology are rapidly changing the nature of French economic and social life.

## Unrest and protest

Unrest is a fact of life in France: people are, it seems, always protesting, whether they be students, fishermen, wine growers, farmers or separatists—Breton, Corsican or Basque—and they are loud and vocal! A few years ago even doctors and travel agents took to the streets to protest against government regulations.

Protesters often express their demands in rather colourful ways, like dumping wine on the road or smashing mountains of artichokes. They can also be extremely violent, as in the Corsican 'vendettas'. Relatively minor, endemic protesting can turn into a serious national disturbance as did the events of 1968. What started as a student riot in Paris swelled into a major confrontation involving ten million people, paralysing the entire nation with strikes, shaking established institutions, and splitting families with dissent.

## The 'average' French person

An 'average' person is not much easier to find in France than anywhere else. However, you can usually expect the French to be relatively conservative in dress and manner and very individualistic—they are not 'joiners'. They tend to shy away from organised activities, which perhaps explains why their political parties and trade unions often splinter.

The French admire intelligence, logic and clear thought, and the ability to express oneself in an articulate, precise and elegant manner. To foreigners they can seem abrupt, intolerant, obnoxious—or perfectly charming.

## Languages and accents

Dialects (some of which are separate languages) are still spoken in certain regions of France: Breton, Alsatian, Basque, Catalan, and Provençal. Many French people speak with regional accents, some of which may be hard to understand.

Differences of speech can also be detected between social groups; the spectrum goes from the refined speech of the university professor to the Parisian popular street language. However, the unifying influence of television can already be heard as more and more French people speak not only with a 'television' accent but use the same colloquial expressions.

On the whole, the French are very critical of how their language is spoken. It even has an institute dedicated to the preservation of the purity of the language—namely, the Académie Française.

## Religion
Most people are Roman Catholic, although religion is not as strong a force today as it has been in the past. About 2 per cent of the population are Protestant and 2 per cent Jewish. There are over a million French Moslems, mostly immigrants from North Africa.

## A LAND OF GREAT CULTURE

Every country is naturally proud of its accomplishments—France is especially so. The French think that most foreigners are abysmally ignorant about France and her centuries-old culture; often they are right.

For the French people, their Culture (spelled with a capital C) is their heritage—works of art, a glorious history of great monarchs and victories on the battlefield, and a succession of famous men and women in the arts, literature and science, provide an intangible bond that ties the French people together, and gives them something that they often get emotional about.

The Minister of Culture has often been a well-known cultural figure, such as the renowned writer and art historian André Malraux. Cultural issues are intertwined with political ones, and a cultural approach is used in political and economic debates. For example, President François Mitterand invited intellectuals and artists to an international conference which was held in Paris in early 1983 to discuss 'Culture, and how Culture can alleviate the world's economic crisis.'

Even the media, especially television, is used by the Government to show how it can promote finer cultural programmes than rival political parties. These are, of course, the object of vitriolic attacks from the opposition. The state of Culture in France is endlessly debated. Some find it too élitist and limited to the privileged, well-educated few, resulting in snobbery and intolerance of other cultures. The French consider their own culture to be a universal message to the world; at the same time, they practise a form of intellectual protectionism. Many important non-French works of history, philosophy and political science were not translated into

French until the 1970s and others are still waiting to be translated
for French readers.

## Accessibility of Culture

The French have done a great deal in recent years to make Culture
more accessible to a greater number of people. Whether socialist or
conservative, the Government has been engaged in an ambitious
construction programme to keep Paris in the forefront of the
cultural scene. The Pompidou Centre (also called Beaubourg) offers
throngs of visitors not only permanent and temporary exhibits, but
also theatres, cinemas, and libraries, as well as workshops and study
areas. The Musée d'Orsay, the totally renovated Louvre, the Picasso
museum, the huge facilities of Paris-Bercy for music and ballet, and
the new opera at La Bastille are but a few of the recent cultural
achievements in Paris.

## Culture in the provinces

Cultural life is no longer the monopoly of Paris. In the provinces
each town has a cultural centre or **maison de la culture** (house of
culture) where classes are taught, exhibits mounted and debates
held. Many of the larger cities have impressive cultural centres.

It seems that each village, church, and château has an arts
festival, usually held in the summer. These festivals allow for
experimentation in creative forms of dance, music or drama.
Performers from other countries are often attracted to them.

## Important people in French Culture

It would be impossible to sum up the great cultural heritage of
France in just a few lines in a book such as this, but learning
something about prominent figures in French culture is rewarding
and wise for those who are to live there. There are some famous
names that everyone should know; the following list is intended as
just a starting point:

Artists:      *Nineteenth century:* David, Ingrés, Delacroix,
              Courbet, Daumier, Corot
              *Impressionists (1870-1880):* Renoir, Dégas, Monet,
              Manet
              *Post-Impressionists:* Cézanne, Gaugin, Seurat, Derain
              *Modern art:* Picasso, Matisse, Léger, Rouault, Braque
Writes:       Molière, Baudelaire, Voltaire, Rousseau, Balzac,
              Hugo, Maupassant, Proust, Gide, Cocteau.

| Musicians: | Gounod, Berlioz, Bizet, Saint-Saëns, Massenet, Debussy, Ravel |
|---|---|
| Explorers: | Cartier, LaSalle, Champlain, Jacques Cousteau |
| Nuclear Physicists: | Becquerel, Pierre and Marie Curie, Louis and Maurice de Broglie |
| Others: | Ampère (electricity), Binet (psychology), Lavoisier and Pasteur (chemistry), Blériot (aviation), Poincaré (maths and physics), Descartes and Pascal (philosophy), Daguerre and the Lumière brothers (photography and films) |
| Famous centres of crafts and skills: | Limoges and Sèvres, porcelain and china; Baccarat and St Louis, crystal; Gobelins, tapestries; Paris, bookbinding, fashion, and furniture reproduction. Many are famous for their wines. |

## THE EDUCATIONAL SYSTEM

The French educational system is excellent at all levels; it is highly competitive throughout, uniformly under state control, and freely available from primary school through to sixth form level. The state has a monopoly on conferring degrees.

The social unrest of 1968 caused a re-examination of many values in France, particularly in education. Since that year, the system has undergone rapid and profound changes. The underlying purposes of recent reforms are as follows:

- to make primary and secondary schools more relevant to the modern world by eliminating rigidity, reducing class size, individualising teaching and introducing new courses and activities.

- To encourage vocational and technical studies by making them more attractive. It is now possible to obtain the **Baccalauréat** (often called the 'Bac') at the end of high school while specialising in technical fields such as computer science or accounting.

- To make the Bac slightly less competitive (65 per cent of the students pass today compared to about 45 per cent thirty years ago) and more accessible by opening a wide choice of 'series' or options.

- To allow more people entrance to higher education by expanding facilities. The small Paris campus of the Sorbonne, established in

1209, has been replaced by thirteen campuses—Paris I to Paris XIII—which serve over 250,000 students. In the provinces many new institutions of higher education have been created to accommodate a greater number of students.

## The Grandes Ecoles

Once the hurdle of the Bac is over, all doors to higher education are open, at least in theory. In fact the competition continues as students are selected out by each end-of-year examination.

Some of the students apply for the uniquely French **Grandes Ecoles** or public institutions outside the university network. Some of these schools specialise in literary subjects, some in scientific, and some in administrative. The graduates of the Grandes Ecoles receive a diploma considered even more prestigious than a university degree. In any event, the selection process is fierce and requires two years of arduous preparation. A student's rank at the end of the school year can determine his or her whole career.

A few of the most prestigious Grandes Ecoles, all located in Paris, are Ecole Normale Supérieure (François Mitterand is a graduate), Ecole Polytechnique or 'X' and Ecole Nationale d'Administration or 'ENA' (Giscard d'Estaing is a graduate).

Graduates of these schools become high-level civil servants and private business executives. ENA graduates who join the corps of Inspection des Finances are guaranteed decisive roles in politics or the public and private sectors of the economy through the French equivalent of the 'old boy network'.

It is easier to understand the people of a country if you know a little about their educational system. Besides, schools and universities are always a good topic of conversation. For more information on the French educational system, see page 109.

## POLITICAL LIFE

French politics can be very confusing for the foreigner—it even confuses the French! Since 1789 France has had a turbulent political history. Its Government has been run successively by a consul, a 'Directory', two emperors, three kings and a 'Commune'. Republics have come and gone; the first in 1792-1795, the second in 1848-1851, the third in 1870-1940, and the fourth in 1946-1958.

### The Fifth Republic
The constitution of the **Fifth Republic**, adopted by referendum in

1958 and inspired by the ideas of General Charles de Gaulle, was primarily intended to put an end to the political instability which had plagued the Third and Fourth Republics. This goal was to be achieved by giving greater powers to the President while curtailing the power of the National Assembly to bring down the Government.

The French system of government is thus a combination of presidential and parliamentary systems. The major decisions, however, are taken at the Palais de l'Elysée (President's office) rather than at the Hôtel Matignon (Prime Minister's office). The central government is divided into three branches: executive, legislative and judiciary (the judiciary is described in detail at the end of this section).

The functions of the executive are carried out by two separate individuals. The **President of the Republic** is the 'head of state'. He appoints the Prime Minister, presides over the cabinet, commands the armed forces and concludes treaties. He may submit questions to the national assembly by a national referendum, and he may dissolve the assembly.

The head of government is the **Prime Minister**. He heads the cabinet. He submits government bills to the parliament and is responsible for their implementation once they have been voted into law.

Of the two legislative bodies—the **National Assembly** and the **Senate**—the former is the most important. The Assembly can overrule the Senate's decisions. It may initiate laws, and by using the 'motion of censure' device, it may also force the government to resign.

In May 1981 the socialists came to power. François Mitterand began a seven-year term as President of the Republic. During this term the two major centre-right groups, UDF (Union for French Democracy) and RPR (Rallye for the Republic), grew in strength. In a gesture of power sharing or 'cohabitation', Mitterand named conservative Jacques Chirac (RPR) as his Prime Minister.

The presidential elections of spring 1988 turned into a duel between Mitterand and Prime Minister Chirac. The socialist President, on the second round of ballots, won over a centre-right coalition for a second seven-year term.

**Elections**

As described above, the President is elected by direct universal suffrage for a term of seven years (before 1965 the President was elected by an electoral college). The President appoints the Prime Minister and his ministers.

The 491 members of the National Assembly are elected for a term of five years by a 'two-round majority' vote. To be elected on the first ballot, a candidate must obtain an absolute majority of the valid votes cast, ie more than 50 per cent of the votes. If no candidates meets this requirement, which is usually the case, a second round of voting takes place the following Sunday for candidates who have received at least 12.5 per cent of the votes in the first round; one candidate is therefore more likely to get a clear-cut majority at this stage. This system contrasts sharply with the pre-de Gaulle system of proportional representation, which fostered the fragmentation of political parties and a perpetually weak and unstable government.

The Senate is the second elected body, made up of 283 senators indirectly elected for nine years by an electoral college.

Elections are an important indicator of public opinion during the long seven-year term of the President. Strangely enough, some of the most important—and most revealing—elections are not for the legislative assemblies at all but for the smallest administrative units of France, the municipality or **commune**. The **municipales**, as these elections are called, give the clearest indication of what people think about the Government, and are closely watched by everyone.

### Political parties

Traditionally France has had a large number of political parties, which are constantly forming alliances that shift with alarming frequency. In addition to the more influential parties (see below), there are a number of smaller ones that rise and fall both in size and importance. The result has been political instability that reached its peak during the Fourth Republic. Today, the French political scene is considered to be rather simple since 'only' four main parties occupy the limelight.

**The Socialist Party** or PS, is currently the largest in France. François Mitterand, Michel Rocard, Lionel Jospin, André Maurois and Laurent Fabius are its leading lights, and its strongholds are in the Nord and Bouches du Rhône districts. Its programme for political reform is based on the following principles:

- Improvement of the working conditions of the labour force.
- An active governmental role in the economy through public investment and the encouragement of research and advanced technology.
- 'Polite' alliance with the Communists.
- Respect for existing agreements with the Soviet Union.

- Completion of existing nuclear power projects followed by exploration for new forms of energy and a new emphasis on conservation.

**The Rallye for the Republic** (RPR), led by Jacques Chirac, bases its programme on the following:

- Complete separation of East and West.
- An independent national defence force.
- Total opposition to Communism.
- Massive investment in the economy.

**The Union for French Democracy**, or UDF, which supports Valerie Giscard d'Estaing (former President), Raymond Barre (former Prime Minister), and Simone Weil (former President of the European Parliament), stresses:

- A confederated but not supranational Europe.
- Acceptance of the Atlantic alliance but, first of all, independence.
- Nuclear deterrence.
- Increased defence spending.

**The Communist Party**, or PC, adheres to the Leninist approach to Communism although it abandoned the idea of 'dictatorship of the proletariat' in 1976. The PC publishes the newspaper *l'Humanité* and acts through the powerful trade union, the CGT.

On the extreme right, the **National Front Party**, or FN, headed by Jean Marie Le Pen, made its appearance on the political scene in 1981. It is extremely controversial, particularly for its anti-immigration position.

### Local government

France has a highly centralised administrative system still based on the original design created by Napoleon Bonaparte in the early nineteenth century. The country is divided into a pyramid of administrative units run by elected local assemblies closely supervised by agents of the central government. The best known and most active of these units are the 96 **departments** managed by **prefects**, who are appointed by the central government, and the 36,000 **communes** led by the **maires** (mayors), who are agents both of the central government and of the municipalities.

Since 1972 efforts have been made to decentralise that system by shifting the power away from the central government in favour of the elected local authorities. In 1972, 22 regions were created which

grouped several departments together. This new regional administration was designed to lessen the role of the central government and
to bring the administration closer to the people. Reforms initiated
in 1982 curtailed the central government's power even more and
gave decision-making authority and a wider area of control to the
various local assemblies: regional councils in the regions, general
councils in the departments, and municipal councils in the
communes.

## THE LEGAL SYSTEM

There are important differences in the legal systems of France and
Britain. France is a **civil law** country, that is, one in which the legal
system is based entirely on a body of written law. Britain is a
**common law** country in which the system of justice depends heavily
on custom and precedent.

Following the principle of the separation of power between the
judicial and executive branches of government as enunciated in the
Declaration of the Rights of Man in 1789, a system of **administrative
justice** applying administrative law was laid down by Napoleon.
This system, originally unique to France, though later adopted by
other countries, is called the **Code Napoléon (Napoleonic Code)**.
Today, 'codes' (or compilations of laws, decrees, and circulars)
govern all branches of French law. There are, among many others,
the **Code Civil**, the **Code Pénal** and the **Code Fiscal**.

France actually has two judicial systems: administrative and
judiciary. The administrative justice system is responsible for settling
lawsuits between the Government and the individual. The system
provides French citizens with exceptional legal protection. Suits are
brought to the 22 **Tribunaux de Première Instance** (Tribunals of First
Instance) and may be appealed to the **Conseil d'Etat** (Council of
State). The Council of State is, incidentally, one of the most
prestigious institutions in France. It also acts as an advisory organ
to the Government on the conformity of proposed legislation with
the body of law.

Running parallel to this system in France is the **judiciary** which
handles civil and criminal cases. The criminal courts include the
**Tribunaux correctionnels** (Courts of Correction), **Tribunaux de police**
(Police Courts), and **Cours d'assises** (Assize Courts), which try
felonies.

Appeals are referred to one of the 28 **Cours d'appel** (Courts of

Appeal). All court decisions are subject to possible reversal by the Supreme Court of Appeals or the **Cour de cassation**.

In English law, the jury system is used in civil and criminal cases. In France, the jury of peers was abolished in 1941. What is called a jury in France is actually a mixed tribunal where six lay judges sit with three professional judges. A two-thirds majority of this 'jury' may convict.

All judges in France are career professionals who must pass a very competitive examination. In criminal courts, the judge has a more active role than is the case in Britain and does most of the questioning of witnesses.

## THE ECONOMIC PICTURE

France is one of the world's major industrial and agricultural giants, with a highly skilled labour force. There has always traditionally been an interplay between Government and economy, which has resulted in price and wage controls, a vast public sector, and a major role for the Government in planning, regulating and subsidising a large part of the economy.

As the Western world's fourth-ranking industrial power, France has a highly developed and diversified industrial sector which employs one-third of the workforce and generates one-third of the gross domestic product. In five key sectors—nuclear energy, telecommunications, aerospace, electronics and transportation—France is at the technological forefront (France has the world's fastest train—the TGV—which reaches speeds of 265 mph). Although known worldwide, perfumes, fashion and films represent a very small part of France's achievements.

France used to depend heavily on imported energy, but through a policy of conservation, use of alternative sources of energy, and a particularly active nuclear programme, the imported energy requirements have dropped to under 50 per cent. In fact the construction of nuclear plants proceeds at a pace considered alarming by ecologists.

### Nationalisation and privatisation

When they came to power in 1981, the Socialists sought to step up the dominant role of the government in the economy. They engaged in a policy of **dirigism**, whereby the nationalised sector would be expanded and include banking, insurance and key manufacturing firms. Since March 1986 and the introduction of power sharing or 'cohabitation' between Socialists and Conservatives, the Government has changed the economic orientation from nationalisation to privatisation and the return of ownership of companies to private stockholders.

## The standard of living
The economic progress of France over the last twenty years has resulted in an abundance of consumer goods. By 1986 statistics showed that 97 per cent of all French households owned a refrigerator, 92 per cent a TV set, 84 per cent a washing machine, 74 per cent an automobile, and 70 per cent a telephone.

## Growth rate
In the 1960s France had a high annual rate of growth, reaching 5.5 per cent, a record surpassed only by Japan among non-Communist countries. In 1974 following the energy crisis, however, the country experienced a deep downturn, reaching its lowest point in 1980. The worldwide recession of the 1990s has hit France hard, causing high unemployment, inflation, big budget deficits, a negative balance of trade, and the need for heavy Government borrowing from international banks.

## Austerity programme
Eighteen months after coming to power the Socialists had to introduce a programme of austerity: deindexation of wages from prices, occasional price freezes, cuts in government spending, and slowing down of imports as well as tighter credits. This policy produced positive results, and inflation fell from 9 per cent in 1983 to below 5 per cent by the end of 1985. Since 1986 the Government has continued the process of fiscal and monetary discipline but has adopted a more market-oriented approach designed to improve the domestic investment climate and enhance France's competitiveness. It has removed foreign exchange and most price controls, reduced taxes, and introduced labour market reforms to favour the employer. But various structural problems continue to trouble the French economy; for example, unemployment remains high.

## Trade
France has long been committed to a liberal world trading system. It is a member of GATT (General Agreement on Tariffs and Trade) and is the second largest trading nation in Western Europe after

Germany. Trade with the enlarged European Economic Community accounts for over one half of French trade. However, within the EEC the Government has been, and remains, a strong advocate of actions to protect weak industrial sectors.

## Anglo-French trade
Up until 1982 the UK was in deficit in its balance of trade with France. However, the increasing purchases of North Sea oil by France gradually changed this situation and in the years 1982-5 the UK enjoyed a small trade surplus with France. Oil prices dropped dramatically in 1986, however, and as a result the UK moved into deficit, a situation which continues today. Nevertheless, there is a steady growth in the UK's non-oil exports to France.

## Labour organisations and management
French unions and federations of unions are numerous but are neither as highly organised nor as powerful as those of her main economic rivals. Union membership, at 22 per cent, is one of the lowest in Europe.

Firms employing ten or more people are required to have **employee representatives** (délégués du personnel), with the limited responsibility of settling individual problems. Companies employing 50 or more people have **personnel-management committees** (comités d'entreprises) to present employee grievances to management and to advise management on matters related to the organisation, operation and management of the firm, which means that the committee's advice is not confined to employee welfare.

## Role and power of unions
The law gives unions the right to organise a **local branch** (section syndicale) in any company with at least 50 employees. There is at least one union branch in about half of all companies with more than 50 employees and in over 95 per cent of those with over 1,000 employees.

Union negotiations are carried out at the national or regional level between major employers' associations and labour organisations. Resulting agreements apply throughout that particular industry.

Labour relations are also based on a **contractual policy** (politique contractuelle), a new concept introduced since the riots of 1968. It provides for renewable and therefore renegotiable labour contracts. This type of collective bargaining is of a broader scope; it determines not only working conditions but the worker's security in a wider social context including retirement, training, and even important matters like the indexation of wages and prices.

## The main unions

The five million unionised workers are split into five leading union federations, which are further fragmented and divided along political lines. In fact many people feel that much of the current labour activity is politically motivated. Most unions are either run by or closely related to political parties.

The largest and most belligerent is the **Confédération Générale du Travail,** or CGT, with 2.5 million members. The leaders are Communist or Communist-affiliated and controlled. They are geographically strongest in the heavily industrialised regions around Paris and Marseille and active in heavy industry, metallurgy, mining, ports, electricity and railways.

The **Confédération Française Démocratique du Travail,** or CFDT, is the most organised and active of the non-Communist unions. It has about 1,100,000 members, most of whom are white-collar workers in the metallurgical, gas and chemical industries. It is strongest in the north, west and east.

The **Force Ouvrière** (CGT-FO) is not connected with the CGT and should not be confused with it. Although it is more moderate in tone, it appears to be supporting leftist unions with increasing frequency. CGT-FO is the leading federation of employees in the nationalised sector and in the civil service. It is strongest in the southwest and in the Paris region.

**Confédération Française des Travailleurs Chrétiens (CFTC)** was founded in 1919 and consists of federations of miners and certain white-collar organisations. It split from the CFDT to continue the tradition of Christian unionism. Its members are drawn from mining, banking, insurance, air traffic control, the oil industry, glass and ceramics. It is found countrywide.

**Confédération Générale des Cadres** (CGC – **cadres** means executives) organises executives and technicians in supervisory positions, and is found countrywide.

**The Conseil National du Patronat Français** (CNPF) represents employers in their relations with the Government and decides to some extent the employers' economic and social policy. CNPF has about 900,000 members in business, industry and banking. It is also found countrywide.

## MANNERS AND VALUES

The French, like all of us, are complex, varied, often contradictory and baffling—only the French seem to be more so. It is always dangerous to generalize, but certain traits of the French temperament will strike the Anglo-Saxon newcomer to that country.

Full of surprises and contradictions, the French will never bore you. They are well known for their adventurous spirit, their flair, their often boastful pride of all things French. The French tend to be impatient (and sometimes intolerant) with foreigners, particularly because of their linguistic shortcomings. Style is paramount to the French and they try to do everything with *panache*—from dressing, to preparing meals, to discussing politics or the weather, even to driving.

Luigi Barzini, in his book *The Europeans* described the French as 'chivalrous, generous, recklessly brave, imaginative, irresistible to women, and above all vain and boastful'. Is it any wonder that the French long ago chose the vain and boastful rooster from all other animals to be their national symbol?

The French love to talk about one of their favourite topics, the grandeur and heritage of France. Like the Chinese, who consider themselves the centre of the world, the French love to say, '*La France est la lumière du monde*' (France is the light of the world). Although some of its grandeur and power have faded, there are valid grounds for French pride. France is still one of the greatest countries in the world. France is preeminent in many fields and is still admired and envied for its culture. The French language is still loved for its elegance, clarity and romance; French wines and cheeses still enjoy an excellent reputation worldwide, and Paris is an important centre for fashion.

In short, France with its old and new splendours, its quarrelsomeness, its warmth and adventurous spirit, its vanity, elegance and flair will undoubtedly frustrate and anger you, but it will also intrigue and delight you.

### Formality and courtesy

The French are still very formal, not only with foreigners but also among themselves. First names are used sparingly. A French person will let you know when he or she is ready for intimacy. If you start right off on a first-name basis, the French don't usually consider it friendliness but rather pushiness, over-familiarity and rudeness. Even one's neighbours can remain *Monsieur* or *Madame* forever.

In France, as throughout Europe, basic courtesy includes shaking hands with people when meeting them and again when saying goodbye (the woman offers her hand first).

Children are taught from a very young age to address adults with the same hand-shaking and the use of *Monsieur, Madame* or *Mademoiselle*. If this simple matter of greetings and departures is done correctly, it can offset a multitude of other 'sins', such as interrupting, barging into a room, not knocking on doors. Many people in France still believe in the old saying that children should be seen and not heard. Some acrimonious landlords will not accept pets or children, although they may tolerate the latter, provided they do not make noise, run, or use the elevator by themselves.

## Privacy

The French are very private people, reluctant to reveal more about their private affairs than is necessary. Personal questions about someone's family, way of life, or even business interests are not considered polite. Safe conversational topics tend toward the latest headlines, books or films, sports, or art.

At work, office doors are kept closed. A phone call is given before an office visit; and then you should knock and wait for an answer before entering. Also, you shouldn't just drop in on the neighbours as in some other countries. To pay a visit, you should be invited, or telephone in advance.

## Change

French society is undergoing many changes. The French have always been known for the value they place on individual differences: '*Vive la différence!*' Uniformity in the way people speak, eat and dress is increasing, however, under the impact of television. As in many other countries, trends in fashion, behaviour, and speech are set by the young. Also, sports and physical fitness are 'in'; even prime ministers can be seen in jogging outfits.

Other, more profound changes are occurring as well. There is a disintegration of many social institutions and the blurring or disappearance of class distinctions. Religious institutions are among those in which this disintegration is most evident. The Catholic Church is losing ground. The number of ordained priests is decreasing (even in western France, the very bastion of Catholicism), and attendance at church services is down, particularly among those between the ages of eighteen and thirty-five.

The working class, with its traditions, culture and geographic base, is also changing. With the closing down of many industries, such as the coal mines, metallurgical industries, and ship building, the working population has been absorbed into other areas. The blue-collar worker has become upwardly mobile—economically if not socially.

But the most alarming trend in French society today, say the sociologists, is the disintegration of the family. A fifth of the children are born to single-parent households. **Union libre** (common-law marriage) is widespread.

Major changes in the social structure result in changes in—and sometimes the loss of—values. *La vie est un long fleuve tranquille* (*Life is a long and quiet river*), a film set in the late 1980s, illustrates this point well. In it a bourgeois family and its values (respect of authority, traditions, hard work and good manners) are caricatured and satirized. In the story its members adopt the permissive and irresponsible behaviour they find in a rival blue-collar, unemployed family. The result is the total disintegration of the bourgeois family.

## Politics

In their attitudes toward political, social or economic issues, the French may also seem full of contradictions. On the one hand, they can passively accept decisions made at the top, such as the construction of nuclear power plants, even though many people are against them. On the other hand, they can flare up at specific problems, such as the state subsidies to private (Catholic) schools in 1984 and university reform in 1986.

Griping, complaining, or criticizing is a favourite pastime of the French. 'They'—that is, the others, the neighbours, the politicians—are always wrong and constitute fair game for biting comments. Politicians are favourite targets.

As a foreigner, talking politics with a French person can leave you shaking your head. The French interlocuter can be alternately brilliant, pontifical, or narrow-minded. A political discussion usually consists of putting down the opposing political parties and tearing to shreds current political figures. Many moderate 'centrist' leaders admire the Anglo-Saxon political system which allows for the alternation of parties in power and the acceptance by the opposition of its momentary defeat.

# 2
# Before You Go

## PASSPORTS, VISAS AND DRIVING DOCUMENTS

Pulling together the documents you need for living and working in France can take longer than you might expect.

### Passports
If you are a European Community national, you can enter France with just a **National Identity Card**. If you are a British national, you will need a valid **British passport**. Your passport should have the endorsement 'British Citizen' (if issued after 1st January 1983) or 'Holder has the right of abode in the United Kingdom' (if issued before 1st January 1983). EC nationals do not require visas.

If you do not have either of these endorsements, usually found on the first page of your passport, contact the French Consulate General in London or the nearest French Consulate to find out whether you will need a visa. French officials often suggest that a personal interview at the consular offices well before your departure date can help you avoid some of the difficulties and long delays which often occur when applying for the necessary papers. **British visitors' passports** may be used for short stays in France, but are insufficient for anything more permanent.

### Short and long stay visas (non-EC nationals)
Short stay visas are available from French consulates and are known as **visas de court séjour**. However, if you are intending to settle in France on a permanent basis, you will need a **visa de longue durée** which will facilitate the issue of a **carte de séjour** or residence permit. It will cost a nominal amount to apply for this, but it does include any children under 16. Apply to a French consulate in the UK; you will need to produce evidence of your financial situation, a medical certificate and possibly some other information about yourself; the

French consulate will supply further information (see **Useful Addresses**). It may take several weeks for the information to be processed, hence the need for an early start in making arrangements.

Non-EC nationals can stay in France for up to 3 months without a visa and this time can be extended with an application to your local **préfecture** once in France. However, to take up permanent residence, you must apply to your local préfecture *with* your visa before you will be granted a residence permit. This will be valid for an initial period of a year, after which you will have to renew it. The initial issue is free; the renewal involves a small fee.

In some cases, a Département official will grant a carte de séjour without the applicant holding a visa de longue durée. It is best to ask your local Préfecture about the policy in your particular area.

For more on residence permits see page 53.

### Working and business in France

Full details about working in France are given in Chapter 4, but at this stage it is worth noting the following:

- If you want to set up your own business in France, you will need a **carte de commerce** to do so. You will then be subject to the same conditions as a French national. For more information contact French commercial or financial services or DATAR (see Chapter 4).

- If you want to practise a profession (doctor, accountant etc) contact the relevant French professional bodies. A French consulate should be able to provide further advice on this; it can be a difficult process.

### Driving papers

To drive in France you need your **national** or **international driving licence**. (If you hold a licence issued in another EC country you do not need an international licence; if your licence was issued in a non-EC country check with a motoring organisation or the French consulate.) You also need your car registration document (known as a **carte grise** in French), if you are taking a car, and an insurance certificate. Though **Green Cards** are no longer compulsory within the EC, it is a good idea to get one, since without it the driver is only covered for the 'legal minimum' whilst driving abroad, which usually means third party. It is also a good idea to obtain a **Driver's Accident Report Form** from your insurance company before leaving the UK.

Once in France, it is advisable *always* to carry your papers as you may be asked for them if stopped by police when driving. At the very least, carry your carte de séjour as a form of identification.

## MONEY

The situation regarding Exchange Control is changing, so if possible check with a French bank to determine what and how much money you can take into France. Basically, it seems that this irritating restriction is being lifted in stages so that any inconvenience caused by it, especially to non-French nationals, will eventually disappear.

### The French banking system
The banking system in France is rather different from that of most other EC countries. It is a good idea to familiarise yourself with the system's peculiarities or you may find certain transactions producing unexpected results! Find out whether your bank has a specialist department with staff well-versed in the banking systems of other EC countries. If not, other British banks in the UK and in France provide such a service, as do certain French banks. Contact local branches for more information.

British people often find that they get on best with branches of British banks in France. You can find these in the provinces as well as in Paris and they are particularly helpful if your French isn't too good and you have not mastered the French way of banking. Also, these non-French banks usually have a much wider international knowledge than most French banks and are likely to have a more flexible approach in general. They are, however, subject to Banque de France regulations and general French banking law and therefore operate very differently from banks in the UK.

### French banks – some useful tips

- When you open an account, confirmation from the Banque de France that you are not under an **interdiction** (see below) is required. This means that there is a central record of all accounts in France.

- The clearing system in France is often slow, so statements are not always an accurate indication of your current position.

- French banks use the 'value date' method; in other words, a cheque paid into your account on a given day will be credited to you on that day but cannot be drawn against until clearance is achieved. This is the same as 'uncleared funds' in the UK, except that bank drafts also need clearing—as though they were cheques.

- It tends to take longer to get a new cheque book than in the UK, so always have a spare on order.

- If you write a cheque with the amount in words differing from the amount in figures, the former will be deemed as correct.

- A cheque is payable on the day of presentation, irrespective of the date written on the cheque, so do not try to use post-dated cheques.

- All cheques must be endorsed. This can lead to difficulties with another person cashing a cheque.

- Usually, all cheques issued by banks are crossed and are not freely negotiable. Open cheques may be issued, but this makes for complications and extra charges.

- If a cheque bounces because of a lack of funds in your account, your bank will send a registered letter advising you of this. You should not issue any more cheques and you must put your affairs in order within 30 days. If a cheque bounces again within 12 months, you will not be allowed to issue cheques for a year and will be required to send your book back. If this happens you are under an **interdiction** and this will have implications for other accounts and for holders of joint accounts. The blocking of an account is reported to the Banque de France who keep the individual concerned on file for 2 years; any violation of the ban is then reported to the police. The ban can then be lifted, however, if you can prove that you were not at fault.

- You can stop a cheque you have issued if you lose your cheque book, it is stolen, or the receiver of the cheques loses it etc; consult your bank if you wish to cancel such a payment.

- Banks in France do not usually pay interest on current accounts. Some banks expect you to keep a minimum balance in your account and, since charges are often high, make sure you know whether a bank makes this condition before opening an account.

- When opening a deposit account in French francs, there is usually a minimum amount payable. The requirements for other currencies, however, can be different so consult your bank manager for this and any other information you need.

- It is not usually a good idea to close your account in the UK, unless you are advised to do so for a particular reason.

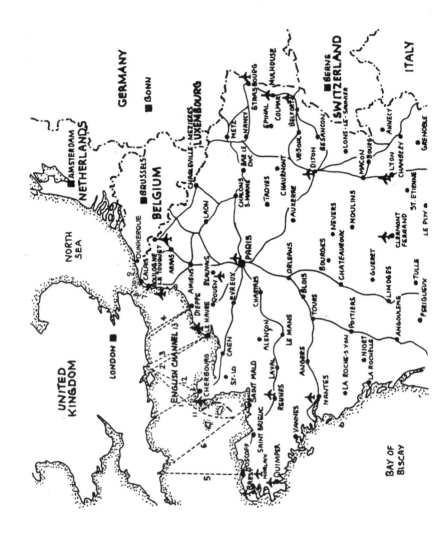

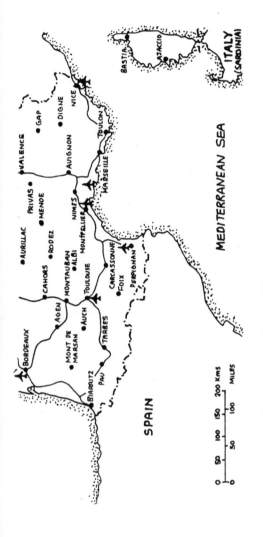

- - - - - CROSS CHANNEL SEA LINKS

1  WEYMOUTH - CHERBOURG
2  SOUTHAMPTON - LE HAVRE
3  PORTSMOUTH - LE HAVRE
4  SEAFORD - DIEPPE
5  ROSCOFF - PLYMOUTH
6  ST MALO - PLYMOUTH
7  FOLKESTONE - BOULOGNE

8  DOVER - BOULOGNE
9  RAMSGATE - DUNKIRK
10  DOVER CALAIS
11  PORTSMOUTH - ST MALO
12  PORTS MOUTH - CHERBOURG
13  NEWHAVEN - DIEPPE

✈ AIRPORTS SERVED BY DIRECT LINK TO BRITAIN

— MAIN RAILWAY

- You don't need to throw away any credit cards you already hold as they should be accepted in France; in fact, such cards are generally more useful than their French equivalents.

## HEALTH REQUIREMENTS

There are no health requirements for entry into France, but periodic checks on travellers make it advisable to carry any certificates showing immunisation dates. Before you leave home obtain European Form E 111 from the DSS in case you need medical treatment. The E 111 confirms you are in the national health insurance scheme, and so entitled to free or subsidised medical treatment in other EC countries on the same terms as residents. Note that E 111s are primarily intended for tourists and are not valid if you go to live in another EC country for more than a year. Some people prefer to take out private health insurance.

## GETTING THERE—SEA OR AIR?

The easiest way for you to travel to France and to your new place of residence within France will depend on a number of factors such as time of year, length of journey and, of course, cost. However you choose to travel, the important thing is to plan everything well before your departure date.

### By air
London is connected to almost all the main French cities. Also, most provincial airports in the UK operate services to France.

### By car ferry
Numerous ferry services are available from Dover, Newhaven, Plymouth, Poole, Portsmouth, Ramsgate and Weymouth. High-speed hovercraft services are available from Dover.

### By rail and sea
Continental services leave from Victoria for Calais, Boulogne and Dieppe. Services for northern, central and southern France run from the Channel ports, although often it is quicker and more convenient to catch a connection through Paris.

Contact the **French Government Tourist Office**, 178 Piccadilly, London W1V 0AL for details of travel routes to France and up-to-date service information. For information on travelling within France, see page 118.

## IMPORT RULES & REGULATIONS

Detailed rules about the importation of household goods should be discussed with the customs section at the French consulate. In general, you can import household items duty free only if your stay in France is to be for a year or more, and if the effects have been in your possession for at least 6 months.

These goods may not be sold for 6 months after entry into the country. Before departure, you will need **un certificat de changement** (change of residence certificate) and an attestation showing that the goods have been in your possession for the required length of time. This document must bear the stamp of a French consulate. To obtain this certificate you must:

- Make an itemised list, in duplicate, of all household effects. You must sign and date it.

- Ask for two declarations of change of residence forms from the consulate which are completed, signed and notarised.

- Visit the consulate, taking along your passport and visa, the lists and the change of residence forms.

### Vehicles

For visits of six months or less you can take your car into France without any formalities. A car may be imported if it has been in your possession for at least 6 months. If you are intending to stay in France on a permanent basis, you will need to register your car in France and the certificate, as well as your driving licence, is required. If you are coming to France to work, you will be liable for a customs clearance duty of 33.33% of the value of the vehicle (new or secondhand). In the case of a motorbike, there are two different rates: 15.6% for bikes of less than 240cc; 33.33% for bikes of 240cc and more. But in view of the cost and bureaucratic hassle it simply may not be worth it.

### Pets

Two certificates are required to import a cat or dog into France:

- a certificate of origin and health;
- a rabies vaccination certificate which must have been issued between 1 and 6 months before entry of the animal into France.

Animals under 3 months of age may not be taken into France. Upon arrival, pets should be registered with the SPCA, 39 boulevard Berthier, 75017 Paris.

## Currency regulations

The amount of French or foreign currency which can be taken into France is not restricted. You are, however, restricted when leaving the country to taking no more than FF 5,000 with you (unless you imported more currency and completed the appropriate form at the time).

## Duty free

With the advent of the Single Market, many of the tight restrictions have gone, and provided duty has been paid in the UK, duty will not be payable by EC nationals on entering France. However, if you are taking in goods via a duty free shop these limits still apply:

200 cigarettes
50 cigars
1 litre of spirits
2 ½ litres of still wine
50g of perfume / 0.25 litres of toilet water
500g of coffee / 100g of tea

## MISCELLANEOUS SUGGESTIONS

The French administration always seems to need birth certificates. It is therefore a good idea to take along translated and notarised versions for the whole family. A supply of passport photos is always useful as they are required for many things.

Make plans early for children's schooling, especially if you want to enrol them in a French school (see page 110).

- Remember when making travel arrangements to France that the holiday season in France runs from Easter to September; it's best to avoid peak periods during this time if possible since flights will be crowded, accommodation more difficult to reserve, and roads congested.

## WHAT TO TAKE

## Clothing

The most appropriate women's outfit for all occasions is the skirt, blouse and jacket combination. The quality varies, but the three-part combination hardly ever does. One rarely sees a daytime dress except for cotton ones in the summer, and trouser suits are not much in evidence. For the major cities you will need some really chic, well-cut outfits. As everyone knows, the French have a flair for clothes. For evening, the 'little black dress' will take you almost anywhere. It is hard to get bras that fit the fuller figure, so take a supply with you.

In general men dress much as they do in most large cities. Men may, however, find that cuts, styles and proportions in clothing tend to be quite different from those they are used to at home, particularly in suits and trousers. Wool suits are fine for all but a few weeks of the year. Sports shirts and conservatively coloured slacks are all right for leisure wear, but the French do not appreciate bright colours or loud patterns in men's trousers. Evening clothes are worn quite a bit. Rainwear is essential, as are warm pyjamas, a dressing gown and slippers.

Both men and women may want to bring a supply of shoes. French shoes are expensive, and many foreigners complain that they cannot find narrow-width sizes. Since there is much to see, be sure to include comfortable walking shoes with springy soles for the marble floors in museums, cathedrals and châteaux. Shoes of this kind also protect against damp or cold floors.

Children's clothing is available and of excellent quality but is quite expensive, and sizes tend to run small. It is hard to find large sizes or wide widths. If your child's school requires uniforms made or purchased locally, then adapt the quantity and type of other clothing accordingly.

There are laundries, dry cleaners, and some launderettes, but prices are high, so take as much wash and wear clothing as possible. You can rent sewing machines quite reasonably (Singer is a standard). If, however, you sew a great deal, take your own machine for they are costly to buy in France.

## Household furnishings

The standard sizes of kitchen appliances and cupboard units are small in France. Keep this in mind—it might be hard to fit a large appliance, like a dishwasher, under the counter. You can buy any kind of cooking pot or utensil in France (probably the best in the world), so you may want to try French cookware.

Many of the apartments may seem drab, so you might want to include in your shipment bright scatter rugs, curtains, pillows, etc. to provide colour. As in all Europe, the tradition has been towards armoires or free-standing cupboards rather than closets built into the rooms. This means that you will welcome whatever storage units—bookshelves, chests, cabinets or bureaux—you take with you.

Wall stripping on which you can set shelves may be an essential if you take many books or much kitchenware. Pegboards for kitchens could be useful.

French pillows may seem hard to you; pillows and pillow cases are likely to be square, so you may wish to take your own. You will not find sheets for king- and queen-sized beds. Curtains, bedspreads and draperies are available.

### Electrical appliances

British appliances will normally work in France as long as you change the plug. The normal voltage in France as in the rest of continental Europe is 220V/50Hz. British voltage is 240V/50Hz, in other words only about 10 per cent more, and with exactly the same frequency. (But note, it may be less easy to use French appliances in the UK since the slightly higher voltage in the UK may lead to overheating in the French appliances). With greater technical harmonisation in the Single Market even these relatively small differences should eventually disappear. You may in any case decide to buy certain appliances once you are in France, or perhaps rent items such as a television set and record player from department stores such as Locatel and Inno.

You might find it convenient to take with you some four-way sockets and just change the plugs at the end of these from British to French, rather than put French plugs on all your appliances individually.

The cost of electricity is high in France. Most houses and apartments are wired for 5-10 amps and so can carry a maximum load of only 600 to 1,200 watts. (You may have to unplug the refrigerator in order to iron, for example). The house can be rewired to carry 20 amps, but watch for overloaded fuses. Current is often stronger near the meter and weaker in the outer rooms.

One last word about appliances: if you bring your own, you could also bring the supplies that go with them—belts and paper bags for the vacuum cleaner, filters for the coffee pot though you'll find most of them are available locally. 'How to' books on small appliance repair and spare parts may also be a good investment since repairmen are hard to find and expensive.

### Personal records

Important financial and property records should probably be left in a safe place at home. However **copies** of all income tax documents for the last four years, records of investments and stocks and bonds, and records (especially your completion statement on your home if it has been sold) should be taken with you to France. Receipts for your moving expenses, especially those not reimbursable by your employer, will be needed for tax purposes.

# 3
# On Arrival

## AIRPORT AND ARRIVAL INFORMATION

Three airports serve Paris: Le Bourget, Charles de Gaulle-Roissy
and Orly. All intercontinental flights and large aircraft use the latter
two. Most international airlines have direct services to Paris.

Charles de Gaulle-Roissy airport is fourteen miles north of Paris
and Orly about nine miles south, but both are about a fifty-minute
drive from Paris. Airport buses leave every twelve minutes for Porte
Maillot Air Terminal (from Roissy) and for the Invalides Air
Terminal (from Orly). There are also public buses and train service
between the airports and Paris. The train ride takes half an hour and
is the cheapest and quickest way to reach Paris. Trains connect with
the Regional Express Métro or RER.

Taxis are available twenty-four hours a day at the airports. If the
taxi driver asks for his return fare, refuse—it is illegal. Car rentals
are also available at all airports. If you drive, take the motorway or
autoroute A1 from Roissy and A6 from Orly. There is also a shuttle
bus service between the airports: travel time is one hour.

## WELCOME AND INFORMATION FACILITIES

Welcome offices (**services d'accueil**) abound in Paris, staffed by
multilingual hostesses who help with maps, directions, hotel and
restaurant reservations, local events and other information. The
central office (**Office de Tourisme de Paris**) is located at 127 avenue
des Champs Elysées, 75008 Paris (tel: 47 23 61 72). It is open from
9h to 22h daily (Note: the French use the twenty-four hour clock;
9.00 am becomes 9h and 10.00 pm is written as 22h). The nearest
métro is located at place de l'Etoile (place Charles de Gaulle as it is
called now).

Other information offices (look for the sign 'i', meaning

42

information) are located at the main railroad stations: Gare de Lyon, Gare d'Austerlitz, Gare l'Est, Gare du Nord, and Gare St Lazare. Central telephone numbers for all five stations are 45 65 60 60 (reservations) and 45 82 50 50 (information).

There is a large network of tourist information offices throughout France. Most French towns have a tourist bureau (**syndicat d'initiative**), which will provide useful information and advice to travellers. They are usually located in the centre of town and are listed in the phone book. The large and well-known cities have tourism centres (**offices de tourisme**).

Each of the twenty-two regions of France also has a welcome information office (**France Accueil**). They can telex for hotel reservations for you in another region. The head office of this chain is at 85 rue Dessous des Berges, 75013 Paris.

Free booklets containing lists of hotels can be obtained at any of the information offices mentioned above. All reputable accommodations are listed, from four-star hotels down to simple hotels with basic comfort. Reservations can be made anywhere in Paris (in the Ile de France, as the Paris region is called) and in the provinces through France Accueil or your travel agent.

Some of the hotels include breakfast in their price. The breakfast, continental style, consists of a choice of coffee, tea or chocolate, and bread or rolls (croissants, if you are lucky) with butter and jam.

A listing of restaurants is also available at tourism offices. It is impossible to list all the places where you can eat in Paris. If you are with your children, you do not have to go to a three-star restaurant to have an omelette or a grilled cheese sandwich. The cafés often serve simple meals: steak, french fries, a green salad and a fruit or piece of cheese.

Official interpreters, wearing armbands to indicate the languages they speak, are fairly easy to find on Paris streets during the tourist season. There is no charge for their help. In addition the French government has been encouraging subway operators, police, and others to learn different languages. French citizens who are willing to help visitors wear a special lapel pin. The tourism offices or your travel agent will provide lists of guides and hostesses in Paris or elsewhere in France.

## GETTING AROUND PARIS

Paris is divided into twenty **arrondissements** or districts. You should know the numbers of the arrondissements; they are essential for

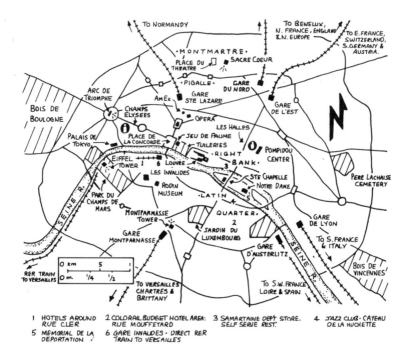

1 HOTELS AROUND RUE CLER  2 COLORAIL BUDGET HOTEL AREA: RUE MOUFFETARD  3 SAMARTAINE DEPT STORE. SELF SERVE REST.  4 JAZZ CLUB · CAVEAU DE LA HUCHETTE
5 MEMORIAL DE LA DEPORTATION  6 GARE INVALDES · DIRECT RER TRAIN TO VERSAILLES

locating where you want to go, and the French refer to them often in conversation.

## Car rentals

Prices for rental cars vary according to the size and make of the car. Automatic transmission or a lockable trunk will cost extra. Added to the price is the 18.6 per cent sales tax (TVA). Rates do not include fuel, which is very expensive in France, or collision or personal accident insurance. Generally, the hirer is responsible for collision damage to the rented vehicle. Always inquire at the time of rental about the cover provided. You can make arrangements to rent a car prior to your departure from the UK through local car rental agents. Airlines will also reserve a car for you. Most large car rental companies have agents at airports and at terminals in town.

## Métro or underground

Paris has one of the world's best underground systems—the métro.

You can get almost anywhere easily. It runs twenty hours a day (from 5h 30 until 1h 30) and is clearly marked, well-lit, quiet and clean. A little time spent with an underground map will reward you handsomely. The basic structure of the métro is a series of concentric circles with spokes at intervals, enabling you to change from one circle to another. One ticket is good for any length trip. It is cheaper to buy a book of ten tickets (**carnet**) than to buy the tickets singly.

## Buses

The bus system is also excellent. The right lane of the streets is reserved for buses, so traffic moves fairly well. Passengers line up at the bus stop (**arrêt**); 'jumping the queue' is frowned upon. Inside the bus is a chart of the route and the stops, with information on how many tickets are needed for each distance travelled. Operating hours vary but are posted at the bus stop. The last bus generally leaves at 21h except for certain lines which run until 0h 30 (12.30 am) in the morning. Bus and métro tickets are identical. Avoid buying bus tickets from the bus driver since it is much more expensive than buying them in the métro. You will need one or two tickets, depending on the distance.

## RER or Rapid Regional Transit

RER (**Réseau Express Régional**) is a new and extremely modern system with underground trains which run deeper than the métro. It is an express system with fewer stops. New lines are under construction which will reach out like tentacles to the suburbs of Paris and eventually serve the entire metropolitan area. Fares vary according to distance, and RER runs from 5h 30 to midnight.

Maps of the three transportation systems are available at news stands, in métro stations, and at train stations and tourist offices. For transportation information telephone 43 46 14 14.

## Carte Orange and other passes

The orange card (**carte orange**) is widely used by Parisians. The card entitles its owner, within certain zones, to unlimited rides for one month on the mass transit system, not only in Paris but also in nearby suburbs. It can be purchased at a Paris métro or suburban railway or bus station. Take a passport picture with you the first time you buy one.

Special tourist passes (**sesame**) are also available for unlimited rides for periods of two, four and seven days.

## Taxis

Taxis are usually white or dark, and there are many of them (about 15,000). But, as in London and other large cities, they are hard to get at rush hours or in bad weather. Cabs are also hard to find at lunchtime as they are often off duty or headed toward their lunch spot. Virtually no taxis cruise in Paris streets. If you want to get one, go to principal street corners or find black and white signs indicating **Station de Taxis**. Another solution is to go to a popular hotel, nightclub or theatre and tip doormen for calling a taxi. However, if you phone for a taxi, the meter will be on when it arrives, as you pay for the trip to wherever you are.

Make sure that the taxi is metered (or your fare may be exorbitant) and that the meter has been properly set back at the start. Day and night rates are shown in each cab and there are standard rates to the airports. There is no charge for extra passengers; some cabs take three and others take four. Tipping is generally 10-15 per cent (20 per cent at night).

If you are going to the theatre or a concert, you may order your cab at the same time you reserve your tickets.

## MONEY MATTERS

### Tipping

There are no hard and fast tipping rules, but generally most service people are tipped: porters, taxi drivers, doormen, room service, waiters, lavatory attendants, ushers in cinemas, cloakroom attendants, hairdressers, etc. Taxi drivers are usually given 10-15 per cent and hairdressers 10 per cent. In restaurants the service is usually included, in which case the cheque will read 'TTC' (**toutes taxes comprises**). It is customary for the customer to also leave small change. Ask a French friend or acquaintance for current amounts for other services.

The concierge at an apartment expects a big tip when a new tenant arrives and leaves, plus one at the New Year, based on the amount of service you have received. Around Christmas or New Year many others will call on you for 'contributions'—the postman, refuse collector, street sweepers, even local firemen.

### French money

Francs are divided into 100 centimes; the franc is abbreviated to FF to distinguish it from both the Swiss (SF) and Belgium (BF) franc.

It is a good idea to get a selection of French money from a bank or money exchange house before leaving home so that all the family can learn to recognize and handle it easily before landing in the hubbub of activity at an airport, with those around you doing everything quickly (and in French). Notes and coins exist in the following denominations:

- Notes (or bills)—50, 100 and 500 francs
- Coins—1, 2, 5, 10, 20, 50 centimes; 1, 2, 5 and 10 francs

The copper 10-franc piece is relatively new. It is quite similar in size and appearance to the 20-centime piece, so be alert not to confuse them.

Currency exchange offices are located in airports, air terminals, railway stations, most banks, and American Express (11 rue Scribe, 75009 Paris, tel: 42 66 09 09; open 9h to 17h Monday to Friday and 9h to noon on Saturday).

### Cheques and credit

Traveller's cheques are the best type of currency to carry when moving around. They are accepted almost everywhere and can easily be exchanged for francs. Remember that when exchanging traveller's cheques for francs, you will get the highest rates at banks or official exchange offices. Hotels and stores usually include a service charge.

Many credit cards are accepted in France, as they are anywhere in the world: Diners Club, MasterCard, American Express, and Visa are well known. Some credit organisations enable the traveller to open a European charge account. The most widely used credit card in France is the **Carte Bleue**, sponsored by a group of French banks. Access/MasterCard and Visa card-holders can use their cards at any outlet displaying a Carte Bleue sign.

Personal cheques may be cashed at any bank anywhere in France provided you use the right type of cheque book — Eurocheques as opposed to the traditional standard British cheque.

### Banking

There are a number of British and European banks in France, but many people choose one of the large French banks. The advantages of a French cheque account are numerous. Personal cheques are accepted everywhere and cheque-cashing outlets are widespread. All you need to show are your ID papers.

You can open a cheque or savings account at a French bank with no formality at all; just show your passport or **carte d'identité**. You will obtain a **compte étranger** (nonresident account), which is an account in convertible francs. You deposit sterling and draw francs. In principle, you cannot deposit francs into this type of account.

After you have lived in France for two years, you will be considered a resident and your bank account will automatically be converted into an internal account.

The largest French banks can issue you the Carte Bleue credit card, which permits holders to cash personal cheques at any bank with a CB sticker. Not all banks honour international credit cards.

French banks do not return cancelled cheques with their statements, so it is important to keep accurate records yourself. Statements should be carefully checked each month to avoid mistakes. (Beware of overdrawing your account, for penalty interest rates are high.)

**Crédit** and **débit** mean the same as in English; **solde** means bank balance, **montant** means total amount. The French use a full stop to separate units of thousands and commas to separate the last two cents (centimes): 400.000,50 is four hundred thousand francs and fifty centimes.

You will notice that French cheques have two dark diagonal lines printed across them: this means that they cannot be endorsed over to a third party. Only the person named on the front can cash it at a bank or savings institution. In the upper righthand corner is a line for writing the value of the cheque in numerals; the line 'payez contre ce chèque' is for writing the value of the cheque in words; 'à l'order de' is the line to write the name of the person to whom the cheque is made payable. The date line is above the signature in the lower right corner.

## PTT (POST/TELEPHONE/TELEGRAPH)

### The postal system
The French postal service is government-owned. A post office handles many more transactions other than post including life insurance, loans (eg for the purchase of a house), the sending of money to someone, buying government bonds, savings accounts etc. You can give long-distance messages to local post offices which will then be sent in writing to people who are not on the phone and you can phone ships at sea. **Pneumatiques** or (*pneu* for short) are written messages sent by compressed air under the streets of Paris and to some suburbs. This is an extremely fast service. **Express** (special delivery)

letters can be sent outside of Paris while **lettres recommandées** (registered letters) can be sent in a number of ways:

- with no receipt requested and no declared value (*ordinaire*)
- with a signed receipt requested (*accusé de réception*)
- with declared value (*valeur déclarée*)

French post offices are usually very crowded. Before joining a queue, be sure that you are at the right window. Postage rates differ with destination as well as with weight.

- It can be helpful to buy a small letter scale and get a list of world-wide postage rates from the French post office. By determining for yourself the correct postage, you can save hours spent queueing.

Main post offices generally stay open from 8am to 7pm, Monday to Friday and 8am to noon on Saturdays. Stamps can be bought at tobacconist's shops as well as post offices.

France uses a 5-digit code system similar to the zip-code in the USA. The first two digits designate the department; the last three the city. Paris is a department in itself and is represented by the number 75; the last three digits in this case stand for an **arrondissement** (district or division). Thus the number for the eighth arrondissement of Paris is 75008.

### Telephones

Pay phones are found in post offices, railway stations, cafés, hotels etc and on the street. There are few coin-operated public phones; most of them now accept only phone-cards—**télécartes**—sold in post offices or tobacconists.

In many hotels surcharges are imposed on calls made from your room. These can be as high as 100%! Avoid this by using a telephone credit card, making a collect call or asking the other person to phone back.

You are now charged a flat rate for each local call, even when using your home phone. Long distance rates vary according to distance and are reduced between the hours of 2200 and 10 as well as on official holidays and Sundays. Rates are clearly explained in the phone book.

For Paris numbers, it is now necessary to add a '4' in front of the former seven digits. When phoning Paris from abroad or from the provinces, insert a '1' in front of the eight digits. If in Paris, you can send a telegram in English at any hour by phoning the PTT (Post/Telephone/Telegraph) on 42 23 44 11.

There are five volumes of the Paris phone book; two with names listed alphabetically and giving telephone numbers for each house number. Consult the pink pages in the front of the first volume for direct dialling information. Direct dialling is now possible to most of Europe and the USA.

If you want a phone installed in your new home there can be quite long delays. Business lines are, however installed promptly, as are phones needed for professional purposes and a medical certificate will give priority to people to whom a phone is essential. Apply for a phone as soon as possible after moving to France to the local **Agence Commerciale des Télécommunications**, the address will be in the turquoise-edged pages of the Yellow Pages. Installation costs will vary, being cheap in a block of flats where a network has already been established and very expensive in remote areas. When you have a phone installed, you will receive a notice. **Ligne mixed** does not mean that you are sharing a line, but that you have both an incoming and outgoing calls facility. If you take over a phone already installed in your home, there is a charge made. You can go ex-directory on request and will be charged a small monthly fee.

If you move into rented accommodation where the phone is in the name of your landlord/lady, you can agree to have the phone registered in your name as end user. In this case, bills will come directly to you. Be certain to cancel the arrangement on leaving or you will still be responsible for the bills.

### Fax and telex

There is a univeral trend towards fax services in France as elsewhere, and these services are now quite widely available. PTT is establishing a public telex service at local post offices. Telexes can also be sent through any of the 'better' hotels. There is a **Post de Telex** at 7 rue Feydeau (2e) from 7h to 23h 30 daily. Tel: 42 33 20 13.

### Minitel

Exciting new technology is entering daily life in France, and **Minitel** is part of it. Minitel is the French equivalent to Prestel. The terminal is loaned, free of charge, to any phone subscriber on request. The terminal, with a computer keyboard, is connected to the phone and allows the users to obtain information (including share prices), to follow a chess tournament, to have access to various data banks, etc. Minitel also serves as an electronic telephone directory and additionally allows the consumer to shop, pay bills, read, and make dinner and theatre reservations. Launched in 1981, Minitel is the largest such system in the world.

## Radio and TV

Television has become a part of French daily life. Practically every family has a set. For someone who has not been in France for a few years, the changes are striking. There are now six channels. The networks broadcast up to eighteen hours a day, and one of the channels—*Canal Plus*—runs round the clock on weekends. There are early morning programmes much as there are in Britain. Competition between the networks is keen. The anchormen and women who present the news and commentary at 13h and at 20h behave like stars and receive enormous salaries.

Until a law was passed in 1982, radio and TV in France were controlled by the state. Since then, some of the stations have been turned over to private ownership, although the government retains some control through a complex system of licensing and a watchdog commission. In order to prevent the weakening of the economic position of the print media, advertising on TV was limited under the 1982 law to 4 per cent of viewing time. Another purpose of the law was to encourage the production of French programmes, thereby reducing the dependence on foreign imports, especially American. Nevertheless, one can't help being astonished at the large number of American films and television programmes—some very old—shown on the French networks.

Two channels are still state-controlled: A 2 (Antenne 2) and FR 3 (France 3). The other four channels are privately owned. TF 1 *(télévision française 1)* is the oldest network. Canal Plus is a pay channel and shows mostly full-length movies, some with the original sound track. La 5 and M 6 (metropole 6) were both created in 1986.

The programmes include variety shows, game and quiz shows, debates and discussions, documentaries, and literary round tables. As an example of the latter, *'Apostrophes'* has been extremely successful. On Friday, at prime time, authors are invited to comment on their work and give their opinions of the work of the other participants.

Foreign television sets (except multi-standard ones) do not work in France because of incompatibilities in broadcast standards and frequencies. You would be wise to either buy or rent a French set after you arrive.

Radio reception is usually excellent and sets are available in France at reasonable rates. There are three main French stations:

- *France-Inter*—round-the-clock programmes on current events, music, discussions
- *France-Culture*—arts and literature
- *France-Musique*—classical music and jazz

Among many other popular stations today are RTL (Radio Television Luxembourg) and Radio Monte Carlo. Shortwave radio is a great pleasure, especially for the wide range of European music it offers and for broadcasts from the BBC. The BBC World Service broadcasts on a variety of frequencies all day and all night. Reception will vary according to your geographical position. Radio Four longwave can also be picked up in many parts of France. You can get frequency charts and programme details from: London Calling, PO Box 76, Bush House, London WC2 4PH. Tel: (071) 240 3406. You can also subscribe to a monthly magazine called *London Calling* for (at present) £10 a year. This gives you a lot of extra information on the broadcasting service.

## The Press
English-language newspapers are available on many news-stands (**kiosks**) each day and include the *Continental Daily Mail* and other leading English-language papers and magazines. One can subscribe to most of these at reasonable rates and have them delivered to home or office. Prices for newspapers, periodicals and magazines may be more expensive than what you are used to.

Brentano's, Smith's and Galignani bookstores specialise in English-language books; however, they are more expensive than books ordered from home and new ones are slow in appearing on the shelves.

A political and literary weekly, the *Paris-Metro*, gives an account of the French press in English (Editions Voudiez, 50 avenue Daumesnil, 75012 Paris, tel: 43 46 13 00).

The French press is extensive; the newcomer is usually struck by the great number of newspapers. No single newspaper has a daily circulation running into the millions as do certain papers in Britain or Germany. But the trend is toward mergers and consequently fewer papers.

The main Paris daily newspapers are (in order of decreasing size) as follows:

*France-Soir*—sensational headlines, mass appeal
*Le Figaro*—moderate right, conservative
*Parisien Libéré*—liberal

*Le Monde*—independent, liberal with leftist tendencies, very serious (few pictures); includes editorials and in-depth articles. Read by intellectuals, both from the Right and the Left

*L'Equipe*—popular readership; emphasis on sports

*Libération*—tabloid, centre-left

*L'Humanité*—organ of the Communist party.

## REGISTRATION AT YOUR EMBASSY

It is a sound idea to register at your embassy soon after arrival. A wealth of information is available there (see chapter 5). Ask to be put on the mailing list of regularly published brochures and announcements. If you have a child born in France, be sure to register the birth immediately to preserve the child's claim to native citizenship.

### Residence Permit

If you intend to stay in France more than three months, you have to apply for a residence permit (**carte de séjour**) within one week of your arrival in France. Except for EC citizens this permit can be issued only if you have been issued a long-term visa (**visa de long séjour**) before your arrival in France (see chapter 2). EC citizens have a right to a residence permit if they have a job in France, or can prove they have the financial resources to support themselves. The permit will normally be valid for five years unless the holder has a temporary job with a contract for a year or less.

The application is made through a welcome centre (**centre d'accueil**)—which is in fact a police station near where you live. Your embassy in Paris has a list of these centres. You must show your passport and provide a local address. You will fill out a questionnaire and then be given a paper showing the date and time (from two to twelve weeks later) when you should appear at the main police department or **Préfecture de Police** (Service des Etrangers, 1 rue de Lutèce, Place Louis Lépine, 75195 Paris).

When you go to the préfecture to obtain the permit, you will need two passport pictures, your passport, proof of financial resources, or the contract with your employer. Your embassy can give additional information and tell you how to renew your permit. It will also tell you about the different types of residence permits available.

## PATTERNS OF LIVING

In France hours of the day are numbered from one to twenty-four; for example 1.20 pm is written as 13h 20, 8.00 am as 8h, and 5.30 pm as

17h 30. A digital watch with a twenty-four-hour option is useful in France.

The standard French working day begins early, usually about 8h but never later than 9h. There has traditionally been a two- or three-hour break at noon or 13h for lunch. The working day then ends between 18h and 19h 30.

In the morning streets are busy as employees go to their jobs and mothers take their young children to school. After rush hour, shopping begins and housewives, shopping bags in hand, go out to buy fresh food for the day in their neighbourhood stores: the baker (**boulangerie**), butcher (**boucherie**), pork shop (**charcuterie**), dairy produce shop (**crèmerie**) and grocer (**épicerie**) (see chapter 6).

At noon mothers go to the school and bring their children home for lunch. They then take the children back to school for the afternoon session. (Schools close on Wednesday afternoon, but are usually in session on Saturday morning). Family dinner is at noon, the main meal of the day.

Although department stores, supermarkets and many other stores are now open all day, small shops still close at noon and do not open again until three or four hours later, remaining open until 19h. Evenings begin late, with supper about 20h or later.

Traffic considerations are causing this traditional pattern to change, particularly in Paris, and the 'continuous day', meaning thirty minutes for a lunch break at a snack bar, bistro or pizzeria, is becoming more common. For many, the working day now ends earlier, freeing more time in the evening for family life or leisure.

In large cities the fast pace of life lasts throughout the day. In the countryside life is slower and days seem very long, with time to stroll about or drop by a bistro for a cup of coffee or a glass of wine. There, almost everything closes for the two or more hours devoted to the midday meal.

The French work very hard during the week, but they never mix work with pleasure. All week they look forward to the weekend when they will be able to potter around the house (do-it-yourself shops are numerous and excellent), perhaps drive to their country cottage (**résidence secondaire**), or have a large family meal (**en famille**) with uncles, grandparents or other members of the extended family. On Sundays they enjoy walking through the parks or the main streets dressed in their best clothes. Sports enthusiasts are seen more and more in their jogging suits or carrying their Adidas bag to a Sunday soccer game.

## ENTERTAINING AND SOCIAL LIFE

Invitations, unless very informal, must be acknowledged by a note or calling card unless otherwise specified. When you are invited to a home, be sure to send flowers ahead or take them with you, especially if you are the guest of honour (not chrysanthemums, since the French associate them with funerals).

Cocktail parties usually begin between 19h and 20h and last two hours or more. Don't worry if you cannot arrive on time. If you are giving a party, try to notify your concierge (in an apartment house) and your immediate neighbours for the sake of courtesy. Even better, invite the neighbours. Large parties should be registered with the police.

Dinner parties are usually at 20h or 20h 30 and you should arrive on time. The French, who love their fine wines, do not like spoiling the taste buds with spirits (although Scotch is commonly served now) before a meal, so do not expect a long cocktail hour.

Formal dinners have several courses: hors d'oeuvre or soup, a fish course, the entrée (**plat principal**), salad, cheese, dessert and coffee. Wine is served with all the courses—white with fish, red with meat and cheese, often champagne with dessert. If you do not wish any wine, you may indicate so by holding your right hand above the glass as the host approaches with the bottle to fill it.

Smoking between courses is definitely frowned upon—the taste buds again. Watch your hostess for the signal to begin eating and start when she does. Often one does not wait for the whole table to be served.

Table settings at a formal dinner may seem a bit different. The silver at the top of the place is for cheese or dessert. A rack or block next to your plate is a knife rest, used when the knife and fork are to be kept for several courses. Again, just watch your hostess to see which silver she is using for each course. Another tip—break your bread with your hands, do not cut it with a knife.

If you are at a dinner party with business associates, you will notice another French custom: business and social life do not mix. There is very little 'shop talk' at the table. After dinner, the men do not remain together to smoke cigars and tell spicy stories. Instead, everyone joins in the general conversation. In the tradition of the eighteenth-century salons, hostesses play an active role in stimulating and sustaining a lively atmosphere.

After any social event or dinner, you should send a thank you note as soon as possible, preferably the next day.

The **concierge** is definitely someone with whom you will want to establish a good relationship. It is the concierge who guards the building, knows everybody's business, handles the mail, and can make life easier (or harder) for all in the house, depending on his/her attitude. A nice tip on arrival is money well spent. Unfortunately, the concierge is a disappearing species, fast being replaced by intercom and mechanical doors.

## LANGUAGE

If you want to get the most out of your stay in France, you simply *must* study French and learn how to speak it comfortably. If you do not, you may find yourself considerably restricted and you will definitely feel left out. As we have said before, the French place a very high priority on their language, and their opinion of you as a foreigner will depend to a significant degree on whether you speak their language. Although they may criticize your less-than-perfect attempts to speak French, they will respect you far more for having tried than if you insist on speaking English.

Schools and institutes teaching French have multiplied, both in Paris and in the other cities of France. Consult the Yellow Pages (**pages jaunes**) of your local phone book. Welcome offices, embassies and consulates, churches, and clubs can provide additional leads. You can also get private tutors or a student to come to supper certain nights a week and help all the family. Another alternative is to go with family members to various activities in the afternoons to improve vocabulary and put yourselves in a French-speaking environment where you will have to listen and speak in French.

Another good way to learn French is to go to a lot of French films and listen to French on radio and TV. Even if you do not understand what is being said, it will help your ear become used to the language, and before long you will be able to pick out single words, then phrases, then the main idea of the programme. Children's television shows can also be very useful learning tools.

When you shop, pay attention to labels—read everything. It will help you learn a lot of useful nouns and verbs, as well as making your shopping much more efficient in the long run. Go to the small local shops for your groceries and learn to order and pay for items you buy. After a while, you'll be able to carry on a simple conversation with the shopkeepers. If you are loyal customers, the shopkeepers will be quite willing to talk and put up with your broken French. Just don't be afraid to try out what you know. You'll both be able to have a good laugh over your *faux pas* in French.

Children or older people in your neighbourhood can also be good helpers. They are two groups in society that always seems to have enough time to chat.

In short, use as many methods to learn French as you can, particularly those fitted to your particular style of learning. And use French as often as you can.

# 4
# Working in France

## GETTING WORK IN FRANCE

If you are a British national or a national of a different EC member country, you are entitled to look for work in France. However, for most public service positions such as the Civil Service, state schools, the Post Office etc, French nationality is required. For other types of employment, here are the ways to go about getting a job.

### In the United Kingdom
If you are experienced or have qualifications in a particular field, it can be worthwhile to advertise in a newspaper. Two addresses through which such adverts can be placed are:

- The French Publishing Group
  15a Elizabeth Street
  London   SW1
  Tel: (071) 730 3477

- The International Herald Tribune
  London Office
  63 Long Acre
  London   WC2
  Tel: (071) 836 4802

If you are an EC national living in Britain and intending to work in France for more than 6 months, you can apply for a job through your local Job Centre or Employment Office. These agencies will give you all the information you need and forward applications, references etc to the French Employment Service, the **Agence Nationale pour l'Emploi**.

## In France

When in France, you can register at your local branch of the official employment service (as above). There are, however, no private employment bureaux in France except the **agences de travail temporaire** which deal only with temporary work.

Other ways of obtaining work in France are as in the UK including personal contacts and newspaper advertisements. Such job adverts will appear in specialised newspapers or journals and in general publications such as *Le Figaro* or *France Soir* (Parisian issues), both of which carry a pretty broad selection of **petites annonces** (classified advertisements).

## SUMMER AND WORK CAMP OPPORTUNITIES

### Summer camps

There are well over 20,000 summer camps in France each year held for children and teenagers. Foreigners seeking paid work as counsellors in these camps normally need the BAFA Certificate (**Brevet d'Aptitude aux Fonctions d'Animateur**). For further information contact:

- **ANSTJ**, Association Nationale Sciences et Techniques Jeunesse, 17 avenue Gambetta, 91130 Ris-Orangis. Tel: (1) 69 06 82 20.

- **CEMEA**, Centre d'Entrainement aux Méthodes d'Education Active, 76 boulevard de la Villette, 75019 Paris. Tel: (1) 42 06 38 10.

- **CPCV**, Comité Protestant des Centres de Vacances, 47 rue de Clichy, 75009 Paris. Tel: (1) 42 80 06 99.

- **STAJ**; 27 rue du Château d'eau, 75010 Paris. Tel: (1) 42 08 56 63.

- **UCPA**, Union Nationale des Centres Sportifs et de Plein Air, 62 rue de la Glacière, 75640 Paris Cedex 13. Tel: (1) 43 36 05 20.

- **UFVC**, Union Française des Centres de Vacances, 19 rue Dareau, 75014 Paris. Tel: (1) 45 35 25 26.

### Work camps

These can be a lot of fun—if hard work—offering summer jobs for volunteers in all kinds of French work camps doing everything from archaeological digs to environmental conservation. The best known organisations include:

- Alpes de Lumière, Prieuré de Salagon, Mane, 04300 Forcalquier: Tel: 92 75 19 93.

- Chantiers Rencontres Internationales, 6, rue Mesnil, 75116 Paris. Tel: 45 05 13 14.

- Compagnons Bâtisseurs, 5, rue des Immeubles Industriels, 75011 Paris. Tel: 43 73 70 63.

- Concordia, BP 238, 27, rue du Pont Neuf, 75024 Paris Cedex 01. Tel: 42 33 42 10.

- Etudes et Chantiers, 33, rue Campagne Première, 75014 Paris. Tel: 43 22 15 61.

- Jeunesse et Reconstruction, 10, rue de Trévise, 75009 Paris. Tel: 47 70 15 88.

- Moulin des Apprentis, Moulin de Piot, Cheniers, 23230 Bonnat. Tel: 55 62 13 20.

- Mouvement Chrétien pour la Paix, 46, rue de Vaugirard, 75006 Paris. Tel: 43 25 49 70.

- Neige et Merveilles, 06430 Saint-Dalmas-de-Tende. Tel: 93 04 62 40 or 93 97 10 39.

## DOCUMENTS YOU WILL NEED

If you are a British national, you need a valid United Kingdom passport which has been endorsed by the British Passport Office with the declaration 'Holder has the right of abode in the United Kingdom'. If your passport was issued after 1st January 1983, the above declaration is replaced with the words 'British Citizen' on the first page.

*NB* a British Visitors' passport is insufficient even for temporary work.

When you go to France, you will be allowed up to 6 months to find a job. Once you have found one, you must apply for a **carte de séjour** or Residence Permit for nationals of the EC member states. This permit is valid for the period of employment if this is likely to last for less than 12 months. Otherwise, it will be valid for 5 years and is automatically renewable. Apply for your **carte de séjour** at the local Mairie or Préfecture de Police. If you are an EC citizen, you will not need a visa to work or set up your own business in France. If you are a British Dependent Territories citizen, a British Subject or fall into any other similar category, you will need to apply to a French Consul in the UK for a Work Permit, **un Permis de Travail**, a commercial card, **(une carte d'identité de commerçant étranger)** and a residence permit. Otherwise, your prospective employer should apply for a Work Permit to the Ministère de Travail (Ministry of Labour) giving details of why you are going to be employed. If you are going to work for a British company in France but do not hold British citizenship, the application for your Work Permit should be made to the nearest French Consulate as it will be dealt with more quickly than those applications made in France. It is not a good idea to enter France as a tourist and then apply for a Work Permit.

*NB* if you are under 18, you will need to produce written consent from one of your parents when applying for work in France. Also, you will not be allowed to work in a bar.

## CONDITIONS OF EMPLOYMENT

Generally speaking, French labour laws apply equally to foreigners working in France and to French nationals.

### Employment contract
Because dismissal procedures are quite complex and lengthy, employees are usually taken on for a trial period of 3 months, during which time either party may terminate the relationship without having to give any notice. Following this trial period, if you have been found acceptable, your employment contract will be written up.

### Wages and salaries
Payment to workers is determined by a statutory minimum wage— the SMIC or **Salaire Minimum Interprofessionnel de Croissance**. This is adjusted each time the consumer price index rises by 2% and at the government's discretion. Also, collective bargaining agreements specify minimum levels of pay for each position within the main employment categories in a particular industry or company.

Most employers pay their workers on a 13 month basis, the extra month's payment being considered a bonus. Banks and some other industries pay the equivalent of as many as 14 to 15 months. The bonus is usually paid in December or in two half-year instalments.

**Professional training**
Companies employing more than 10 people are required to provide job-related training known as **formation continuée** to those employees who want it. This applies to foreign as well as French companies.

**Working hours and holidays**
The average working week is 39 to 39.5 hours and maximum working hours are legally defined in most industries. The law also demands that you should be paid overtime rates for any hours worked beyond the relevant normal working week; this rate being 125% for the first 8 hours and 150% thereafter.

The minimum statutory holiday entitlement is 5 weeks with the addition of the following official holidays:

- New Year's Day
- Easter Monday
- Labour Day (May 1st)
- Ascension Day (10 days before Whitsun)
- Pentecost (50 days after Easter)
- National Day (July 14th, Bastille Day)
- Assumption Day (August 15th)
- All Saints' Day (November 1st)
- Veterans' Day (November 11th, Armistice Day)
- Christmas Day

All public offices are closed during holidays and only the most essential work is done. Many people add some of their holiday time to official holidays to make long weekends throughout the year.

The majority of French workers seem to take their annual holiday during August. At this time, whole factories, shops and offices shut down and there is a mass movement of people across the country. The government is trying to encourage the staggering of holidays because of the adverse effect on business of this mass exodus, but the response has been poor.

## EMPLOYEE BENEFITS

France has a highly developed system of social legislation. The cost of the various benefit schemes is met by employee and employer contributions (in the proportion of roughly 1:3). The main benefit programme is called **Sécurité Sociale** and all paid workers living in France and their dependants are automatically enrolled. The benefits include pensions (retirement, disability, survivor's), wage replacement benefits, medical benefits (see Chapter 7), family allowances and working people's compensation. Leaflet SA29 from the DSS details 'your social security, health care and pension rights in the European Community'.

In addition to the more formalised benefits, a number of optional or non-compulsory benefits are frequently offered: cafeteria facilities, housing and medical check-ups. Top executives can expect company cars and club memberships.

To supplement the standard benefits, many companies provide private benefit coverage. Such coverage is usually more extensive and generous for managerial and executive personnel than for other employees.

## LABOUR ORGANISATIONS

French unions and federations of unions are numerous but are neither as highly organised nor as powerful as those in other Western countries. Union membership, at 22%, is one of the lowest in Europe.

Firms employing 10 or more people are required to have **délégués du personnel** (employees representatives) who have some power in settling individual problems. Those companies employing fifty or more people have personnel-management committees, **comités d'entreprises**, to present the grievances of employees to management and to advise management on matters related to the organisation, operation and management of the firm. The advice given by these committees is therefore not confined to employee welfare.

### The role and power of unions

The law gives unions the right to organise a local branch known as a **section syndicale** in any company which has at least 50 employees. There is at least one union branch in about half of all companies with this minimum number of employees and in over 95% of those with over 1,000 workers.

Unions represent employees in negotiating collective agreements— **conventions collectives**—and have certain rights within companies. Such negotiations are carried out at national or regional level between major employers' associations and labour organisations. Resulting agreements apply across the particular industry.

Labour relations are also based on a contractual policy, **politique contractuelle**, a new concept introduced since the riots of 1968. This provides for renewable and therefore negotiable labour contracts.

This type of collective bargaining is of a broader scope than previous arrangements; it determines not only working conditions but the worker's security in a wider social context including retirement, training and even indexation of wages. The principal unions in France are as follows:

- The **Confédération Générale du Travail** is the largest union with 2.5 million members. It is strongest in the heavily industrialised regions around Paris and Marseille and active in heavy industry, metallurgy, mining and railways.

- The **Force Oeuvrière** is the leading federation of employess in the nationalised sector and in the civil service. It is strongest around Paris and in the south west.

- The **Confédération Française des Travailleurs Chrétiens** was founded in 1919 and consists of federations of miners and certain white-collar organisations. Its members are drawn from mining, banking, the oil industry, insurance, air traffic control and ceramics. It is found countrywide.

- The **Confédération Générale des Cadres** organises executives and technicians in supervisory positions. It is found countrywide.

- The **Conseil National du Patronat Français** represents employers in their relations with the government and has some influence on companies' economic and social policies. There are about 900,000 members in business, industry and banking. It is also found across the country.

## TAXATION

The French system of taxation is complex. The state derives most of its tax revenue from turnover taxes, especially the TVA (VAT). Company income taxes provide 9.9% and individual income taxes only 19.9% of government revenues.

The basic rules governing taxation in France are as follows:

- All **individuals**, whether French or foreign nationals, considered to be resident in France for taxation purposes, are taxable on their world income. A person is deemed to be domiciled in France if he or she has a home there, spends most of the time there, carries on professional activity there or has his or her centre of economic interests there.

- French and foreign **companies** are generally taxable only on income from French sources, according to the principle of territoriality.

## Individual taxation

People resident in France enjoy one of the lower rates of income tax in Europe.

Taxation rates are limited further by a series of deductions, reductions and credits. These include: alimony and child maintenance payments, payments to dependants needing financial assistance and to adult children not regarded as dependants, charitable donations etc.

## Taxation of foreigners

The present system was set up to alleviate double taxation, which plagued foreign citizens living in France before 1979. Tax credits **(avoir fiscal)** are allowed by each country for a portion of the taxes imposed by the other country.

Foreigners not permanently domiciled in France are taxed only on their income from French sources or on the basis of three times the rental value of their real property in France, whichever is higher. (This applies to French citizens as well.)

Everyone who is a resident of France for more than 183 days must file a French income tax declaration. Foreigners resident in France are subject to a progressive and heavy income tax on their personal income.

The personal income tax of all members of the family is generally reported and paid by the head of household. A system of income splitting applies: each parent counts one unit, each child half a unit. The total taxable income is divided by the number of units.

Before leaving France, foreign employees must obtain a tax clearance or **quitus fiscal**.

A very useful organisation is DATAR, **Délégation à l'Aménagement du Territoire et à l'Action Regionale**. This is an interdepartmental economic agency producing publications on the French system of taxation, tax incentives, company law, doing business in France and other related subjects. The address in the UK is:

DATAR
21-24 Grosvenor Place
London   SW1X 7HU
Tel: (071) 235 5148

The publications seem to be largely intended for those with their own business or who plan to set one up. However, information on the French tax system should be invaluable to anyone intending to live and work in France. The address of DATAR in France is:

DATAR
1 avenue Charles Floquet
75007 Paris
Tel: 47 83 61 20

## UNEMPLOYMENT IN FRANCE

Already mentioned is the leaflet SA29 obtainable from the Department of Social Security in the UK. This leaflet gives extensive information on all aspects of social security benefits and allowances in European Community countries. For information above and beyond that provided in this booklet, write to the following address:

Department of Social Security
Overseas Branch
Newcastle-upon-Tyne
NE98 1YX

# 5
# Doing Business
# In France

## BUSINESS PRACTICES

### Business etiquette

Just as manners and clothes are conservative in France, so too are business practices—especially in secondary cities like Lyon or Bordeaux, which tend to be more traditional than Paris.

Business interviews should not be rushed. General conversation often precedes business talk. Most French business people have a wide variety of interests—theatre, opera, art, sports, travel—and enjoy conversation about common, nonpersonal interests before getting down to business. The French also like to take their time in closing business deals and may freeze up if rushed. The hard sell is definitely *not* appreciated. Considerable deliberation is part of the process and decorum is the rule. Appointments are a must in the French business world, preferred times being midmorning and midafternoon.

The French prefer not to mix business and social occasions. Business lunches are not appealing to them. They enjoy invitations to dinner, but to talk business over a good meal is sacrilege! The rule of thumb is to avoid talking business on all social occasions.

Which languages to use in conducting business in France is an important consideration. If you do not speak French well, it is better to do business in English through an interpreter. There are many nuances and/or shadings in French which foreigners often have difficulty in understanding. Most French business people speak English, and those who do (especially top executives of large firms) are fluent and like to use it. However, even though you may be able to converse with your French counterparts in English, it is best to translate correspondence, catalogues, promotional materials, export documents etc into French and to use metric weights and measures.

## Investment climate

The French government has continued to encourage foreign investment in an effort to create employment and attract high-technology industries. It offers tax incentives, loans, financial assistance, land at reduced prices, and other incentives, particularly when the industrial facilities are to be established in depressed or less developed areas. The interdepartmental economic agency DATAR (**Délégation à l'Aménagement du Territoire et à l'Action Régionale**) implements this policy of investment incentives. The US remains by far the most important foreign investor, followed by Switzerland, Germany, the UK, The Netherlands, Italy and Sweden.

## Red tape

Red tape is legendary in France. If you have to redeem a railway ticket, lodge a complaint, or try to change a bill of lading—any official bureaucratic transaction—you will be shunted from window to window and floor to floor and asked to fill out form after form. Part of the reason for the formidable amount of red tape is the fact that the government is the primary employer; there are a staggering number of civil servants. The state practically has a stranglehold on the country's economy since it controls a large share of all commercial activity.

The French people are the first to complain about the frustrations caused by cumbersome and sometimes senseless procedures. But they also know how to laugh about endless bureaucratic tie-ups, and they continuously caricature **fonctionnaires** (civil servants or bureaucrats) in plays and novels. Often you will save time and aggravation if you give a French employee time off to deal with the bureaucracy for you.

## WORKING HOURS, HOLIDAYS AND PUBLIC HOLIDAYS

**Working hours** (Monday-Friday)

- Government:    9h-12h and 14h-18h
- Banks:         9h-12h and 13h 30-16h 30 (closed for a half day before all legal holidays)
- Commercial    8h-12h 30 and 14h 30-17h
  Offices:

Note: The above schedule may be slightly altered by the relatively new thirty-nine-hour work week. Be sure to check hours at each office before visiting. Fuller details are given on page 62.

## SPECIAL SERVICES TO ENGLISH-SPEAKING BUSINESS-PEOPLE

Most of the services described below are available to all English-speaking nationals living in France.

### The British Embassy
The British Embassy in Paris (see reference section at end of book) can provide valuable information on such things as:

- lists of law firms, tax specialists and accountants,
- lists of British banks,
- lists of insurance companies,
- general information about French administrative regulations such as permits, driver's licence, taxes, and dependants' employment,
- principal Franco-British organisations in Paris.

The commercial section of the embassy puts out a number of publications helpful to businesspeople on the investment climate, human resources, trade, and so on. You can also get a list of licensed interpreters and translators. Also consult the Yellow Pages of the phone book under *professions traducteurs-interprètes*.

### The British Chamber of Commerce
The British Chamber of Commerce (see end of book for address) has lists of all the British companies in France and a large amount of other useful business information.

### Services offered by leading accountancy firms
A number of international accountancy firms with representatives in France regularly publish brochures on doing business in France, dealing with taxation, banking, foreign exchange controls, social legislation, etc. To name but a few of those:

Deloitte, Haskins and Sells—Tour Franklin, 92080 Paris La Défense; tel: 47 74 50 12

Price Waterhouse—8 place Henri Bergson, 75008 Paris: tel: 42 94 16 16 telex: 641873

Blanchard Chaveau et Associés—Tour Maine-Montparnasse, 23 avenue du Maine, 75015 Paris; tel: 45 38 22 22; telex: Paire A 200138F

Touche Ross and Co.—185 avenue Charles de Gaulle, 92200 Neuilly-sur-Seine

## Services offered by the French Government

A section of the French government tourism office—France Congrès and Comité Parisien des Congrès (24 avenue de l'Opéra 75001 Paris; tel: 42 96 03 78 or 42 96 03 61)—is devoted entirely to business visitors during their stay in France. The nonprofit association was created to help all those responsible for the organisation of conventions, conferences, symposia, sales meetings, or exhibits. It provides a choice of conference facilities and accommodations, as well as an opportunity to enjoy the cultural or gastronomic attractions of the area. A *France Congrès Newsletter* in English is sent on request if you write to the address above.

DATAR is the French government agency which provides assistance to foreign investors who wish to create or expand their operations in France. It provides a wide range of information in such areas as human resource management and legislation. DATAR (1 avenue Charles Floquet, 75007 Paris; tel: 47 83 61 20; telex: 200970) issues periodic reports on doing business in France, foreign investment in France, investment incentives in France, multinationals, and other subjects. For the UK address see page 65.

## WORKING CONDITIONS

It is important for a foreigner living and working in France, whether an employer or an employee, to be aware of current working conditions. A brief description of the main points follows. (DATAR, in its publication, *Human Resources Management in France*, provides more information on working conditions and its services to business people in France.)

### Employment contract

Because dismissal procedures are quite complex and lengthy, employers usually engage recruits for a trial period of three months during which time either party may terminate the relationship without notice. Following the trial period, if the new employee has proved acceptable, the employer writes up an employment contract.

### Professional training

Companies with more than ten employees are required to provide job-related training (**formation continuée**) to employees who wish it. This also applies to foreign companies.

## Direct remuneration

Salaries in France are influenced by a statutory minimum wage or SMIC (**Salaire Minimum Interprofessionel de Croissance**), which is adjusted automatically each time the consumer price index rises by 2 per cent. In addition to this overall minimum salary, collective bargaining agreements specify minimum levels of remuneration for each position within the main employment categories.

Most companies pay their employees on a thirteen-month basis, the extra month's salary considered as a bonus. Banks and some other industries pay the equivalent of as many as fourteen to fifteen months. The bonus is usually paid in December or in two half-year instalments.

## Employee Benefits

A summary of employee benefits is given on pages 62-63. In addition to the more formalised benefits, a number of optional non-compulsory benefits are frequently offered as well: cafeteria facilities, housing and medical checkups. At the top executive level, the high-status benefits are the company car and club memberships—considered part of the salary.

To supplement the standard benefits, many companies provide private benefit coverage. Such coverage is usually more generous and extensive for managerial and executive personnel than for other employees.

In 1967 the government issued ordinances instituting a plan for compulsory profit sharing (or participation) in all private companies with one hundred or more employees. A substantial portion of the cost of the employee profit sharing is in fact borne by the government, since the share of profits allocated to the employee is tax deductible for the employer.

## BUSINESS TAXATION

The state derives most of its tax revenue from turnover taxes, especially the TVA (value added tax), which brings the government 42.7% of its revenues. Company income taxes provide 9.9% and individual income taxes only 19.9% of government revenues.

Traditionally, the French have been skilled at tax avoidance. Over half of French companies report no profit to the tax assessor. French tax laws are codified in the General Tax Code (**Code Général des Impôts**).

- French and foreign companies are generally taxable only on income from French sources, according to the principle of territoriality.

## Corporate Tax

Industrial or company profits are taxable in France if the enterprise is engaged in business activity through a permanent establishment in France.

The standard rate of corporation tax (**impôt sur les sociétés**) is 45%. It is paid on income before distribution of profits. Net short-term capital gains are taxed at 50% and long-term capital gains at 15% (25% for building land and 10% for commercial professions) provided they remain invested in the company.

## Tax incentives

Tax incentives are widely used to facilitate restructuring of various economic sectors and to redress the imbalance caused by industrial concentration in the Paris region. These include

- exceptional depreciation deduction of 50% given for (1) research, water treatment, air pollution control, or activities contributing to the development of industry, trade and agriculture and (2) the transfer, creation or extension of industrial or commercial enterprises in the less developed areas of France;

- favourable treatment of gains made in mergers;

- the opportunity for companies which maintain or increase their staff levels to deduct a portion of their profits;

- the opportunity for individuals to deduct from their taxable income the cost of certain purchases of shares in French companies.

## Tax on Added Value

Probably the most odious tax for anyone living in France is the tax on added value, or TVA. It is levied on all transactions involving supplies of goods and services. (Exports from France are not subject to the TVA.) The rates are graduated according to the degree of necessity and usefulness of the product, the highest rate being applied to luxury items:

- **super-reduced rate**   5% on food products
- **reduced rate**   7% on books, transportation, hotel services, theatre tickets, medicines, etc.
- **standard rate**   18.6%
- **increased rate**   33.3% on luxury items (furs, perfumes, cars, cameras, tobacco, etc)

## Other taxes

There are a number of registration and recording taxes. Local taxes are levied by the state for the benefit of the departments and communes. These include a real estate tax (**taxe foncière**) and a residence tax (**taxe d'habitation**).

The whole matter of taxation is very complex, and regulations change often. Professional advice may be essential.

## FRENCH COMPANY LAW

A French company is considered to be under nonresident control when more than 20% of its capital is foreign-owned. Foreign investors have a choice of two forms for their business enterprises: (1) They may create a branch (**succursale**), which is not a legal entity. A branch is more convenient when a noncommercial function is planned. The parent company has unlimited responsibility for the debts incurred. (2) Alternatively, they may purchase or constitute a company or create a subsidiary (**filiale**).

The two types of companies most frequently used by foreign investors are as follows:

- The **société anonyme** (SA) is similar to a British limited company. The creation of an SA requires seven members who may be alien or French. Minimum capital is 250,000 FF. The SA is managed by a board of directors (**conseil d'administration**) and a **président directeur général** (PDG).

- The **société à responsabilité limitée** (SARL) is also a limited liability company with certain features of a partnership. A SARL may be formed with a minimum of two members and a maximum of 50, aliens or French, with a minimum capital of 20,000 FF. It is managed by one or several managing directors (**gérants**). The main advantage of a SARL is that it involves fewer formalities and is less expensive than an SA.

## FOREIGN EXCHANGE CONTROL REGULATIONS

**Direct investment** is defined as (a) the purchase of a business or the establishment or expansion of a branch or subsidiary and/or (b) all other transactions which enable one or more persons to increase control of a company.

A nonresidential investor who wishes to make a direct investment in France must file a prior declaration with the Directorate of the Treasury (**Direction du Trésor**), the Ministry of the Economy, or with the Banque de France if real estate business is involved.

Nonresidents can open nonresident French franc bank accounts; only foreign currency can be deposited. Foreign nationals who take up residence in France retain the status of nonresident for two years. After this period, however, they are considered residents and all regulations covering residents apply. Their nonresident bank account is automatically converted into an internal account.

Foreign nationals resident in France become nonresidents as soon as they leave France permanently and at that time may transfer all their assets abroad.

Good sources for initial information on taxation, labour and social security law, foreign exchange regulations, and other matters discussed above are free brochures periodically issued by the British Embassy, DATAR, and law and tax consultant firms, such as Deloittes, Price Waterhouse, and Touche Ross.

## DEPARTMENT OF TRADE AND INDUSTRY INFORMATION

The France country desk provides a wide range of market information free of charge to British exporters. The information which is available in hand-out form includes:

*Tariff Statements*
*Temporary Import and Samples*
*Labelling, Marking and Packing*
*Textile Labelling*
*Foodstuffs Labelling*
*Foodstuffs – Food Additives*
*Lawyers and Debt Collection Agencies*
*Exchange Control*
*Mail Order*
*Agency Legislation*
*Manufacture Under Licence*

*French Government Buying Procedures*
*UGAP (French Government procurement body)*
*Law Number 75-1349 of 31 December 1975 on the use of the
  French language*
*Marketing Consumer Goods in France*
*Selling to Western Europe*
*Marketing Consumer Goods in Western Europe*
*Advertising Agencies*
*Forming a Company in France*
*Lawyers*
*Accountants*
*Personal Selling*
*Some Notes for British Firms Performing Contract Work Using
  their own Staff, Materials and Equipment*
*Warehousing in France*
*Estate Agents and Surveyors*
*Translation of French Customs bulletin on TVA recovery*
*Booklet, 'Mail Order in France'*

For the DTI address, see page 141.

Bimonthly full colour magazine available free from the Invest in France Bureau, 21-24 Grosvenor Place, London SW1X 7HU, Tel. (071) 823 1895. Full of up to the minute national and regional trade information and contacts.

A detailed and lavishly produced guide to investment opportunities in France, region by region. Extra large format paperback, fully illustrated in colour, and packed with local information and advice. Free from Invest in France Bureau (see opposite).

# 6
# Your Home in France

Once you have decided that you wish to move to France, one of the most important points to consider is where you want to live. A possible way to start might be to look at Chapter 1 which gives details on variations in climate and terrain of the different areas of France. France is a lot larger than Great Britain and there are quite extreme differences between environments to consider. Your reasons for moving to France could also influence your choice; an area suitable for those retiring from their jobs may not be as appropriate for a couple with a young family, for example. Also, remember that a place you have visited on holiday for a couple of weeks at a time may not be quite so charming to inhabit all year round.

## AREAS POPULAR WITH BRITISH PEOPLE

Settling in an area where some fellow British have already established themselves may help you to get used to your new home. A small but well established British community is to be found in the north west of France, with another between Bordeaux and the Spanish border. In recent years the Côte d'Azur and the Dordogne have also become popular.

Figures compiled to show the numbers of people buying property in France indicate that the greatest influx of non-French has been occurring along the coast between Marseille and Menton; in the Var and Alpes Maritimes. However, patterns of this nature may change with the opening of the Channel Tunnel when other areas of France will become more readily accessible to the British.

## REGIONAL PRICE VARIATIONS

One needs some guidelines on the relative expense of accommodation across France. As in Britain, the price you pay for a quite luxurious house of considerable size in one region may only buy a poky little flat in another. Anyway, here are some pointers which may be helpful:

- One of the most expensive areas of the country outside Paris is Cannes, followed by parts of Nice, Villefranche and Beaulieu.

- Prices in the Alpes Maritimes are in a league of their own, being more expensive than Paris.

- Both Antibes and Menton vary widely in terms of accommodation prices, though Menton includes Roquebrune–Cap Martin which is a very sought after and therefore expensive area.

- St Tropez and surrounding areas are very expensive, the prices gradually falling as you go inland.

- As you might expect, older property in most regions tends to be cheaper, though the initial low cost may be offset by the expense of renovation (see **Renovating older properties** below).

## DIFFERENT SORTS OF ACCOMMODATION

As you might expect in a large western country like France you can choose from quite a variety of different 'set ups' in terms of accommodation. Even if you are going to be working in a major city, the **RER** (a rapid transit system) means that you can still live in quieter, less densely populated areas and commute to work. Here are some examples of styles of accommodation you might encounter:

- An **ensemble** of apartment buildings situated within a park with sport and shopping facilities and sometimes even a school. Most such ensembles tend to be found in Parisian suburbs but the idea is spreading to other areas.

- Occasionally you might come across **parc residences**, formerly large estates subdivided into private homes. Such areas might even include a château and each home may have its own private grounds complete with swimming pool and tennis court! Such residences are, needless to say, expensive.

- Around Paris, Levitt villages are to be found. These villages are made up of thousands of American-style houses which have been built by an American company. This idea has now been copied by other companies including the British Bell Company which constructed the Parc du Château de Montebello near Paris.

- In Paris itself there are charming older buildings as well as stylish new ones. The French are traditionally a nation of flat-dwellers: in many areas flats are the only accommodation—to buy or rent—available. Such housing tends to be expensive, especially if located in the better areas particularly of central Paris. The cities seem to be congested places to live, especially in medieval towns which developed when the population was much smaller.

## Renovating older properties

Old houses can be full of character and charm but they are likely to be poor in terms of home comforts. If you decide to buy such a property with a view to renovating it, you should bear in mind that problems associated with any work like this are likely to be magnified in a foreign country where unfamiliarity (for example with Building Regulations) and language problems can cause difficulties.

## DIFFERENT WAYS OF BUYING PROPERTY

The most common ways of buying property in France are as follows:

### Outright Purchase

Unlike the arrangements in the UK, there are no 'freehold' or 'leasehold' properties in France. Instead, there is a distinction drawn between **co-ownership** and a **free standing** property.

- If a property is co-owned, it is divided into units. Each unit has a private area and a proportion of the communal area. There are various co-ownership regulations called **Le Règlement de Copropriété** which govern boundaries between exclusive and communal areas, conditions for use of the building etc. Other matters associated with such schemes are covered by an assembly of co-owners called a **Syndicat de Copropriétaires**.

- If you are not involved in a co-ownership scheme but are buying your property independently, you will have all the rights of ownership. You can apply for a mortgage, though managing, selling or leaving the property to someone will all be subject to French law. You are not responsible for any debts left by the previous owner of your property.

- The above will be different if your property is bought through a company, when there will be tax implications.

- Temporary ownership usually involves a building lease; this is a rare arrangement and involves the services of a specialist consultant. More often, properties are sold using a **nouvelle propriété**, an agreement lasting at least nine years.

## Time share

Here, you buy shares in a property owned by a company. This will entitle you to occupy the building according to stipulations set down by the company. Be sure to examine the company's Articles of Incorporation—regulations covering its organisation and how its business is conducted. It is best to stick to a company restricted to buildings where most units are already reserved and to buy at 'low season' times (ie away from Christmas, Easter etc) since prices are set according to demand which is high during 'high season' times.

## Location vente (purchase by instalments)

This method of buying property has been very popular in France over the past 40 years or so and can be very convenient if you cannot afford the outright purchase of the building you want. The method works as follows:

- The vendor company **lets** the building in question to you.

- Attached to your lease you are given a **promesse unilatérale de vente**, a unilateral promise to sell.

- When you deposit a sum of money, you will receive a contract offering you immediate accommodation and the chance to buy your residence at the end of a certain amount of time.

- Any money you pay during this time will go towards the purchase of the property.

One of the main attractions of this sort of arrangement is that it allows you as a potential purchaser to become familiar with a building, to discover any problems etc before actually committing yourself.

- The period of your let will usually be between 2 and 3 years;

- The deposit will be between 3% and 5% of the full price;

- The rent payable will be higher than average for your type of accommodation;

- If you decide after entering into such an arrangement that you do not want to buy your accommodation, you will lose all the money you have paid up to that point.

## Achat en viager (life annuity purchase)

This can be a rather risky way of acquiring property and as such is rarely used. Such a document combines two contracts: one for the sale of the property and one for a Life Annuity for the vendor or crédirentier (the beneficiary of the annuity). The life annuity is a sum of money paid to you—the **débirentier**—to the **crédirentier** until the latter dies. The amount you pay will be assessed by the Notaire (see section on **Notaires** later on) according to the life expectancy of the crédirentier.

## Uncompleted property

If you want to buy a property which is still being built, you will usually do so **sur plans** or on sight of the blueprint. Such a purchase is governed by legislation covering sale of properties under construction.

There are two types of contract which may be used. The first is known as **Term Sale** but is very rare and so will not be discussed here. The second is called sale in the **Future State of Completion**. With this type of contract, the vendor agrees to have the building finished within a certain length of time, whilst retaining control of the works. On completion of the property, rights over the building and its land are turned over to you. You in turn agree to pay for the property as work progresses.

A preliminary contract will be drawn up before the final deed is signed. This is known as a **contrat de réservation** or option agreement and should cover the following:

- The purchaser pays a deposit of between 2 and 5% of the cost of the building.

- There is a guarantee of satisfactory completion of the building.

- There is a guarantee against defects for a period of 2 years.

- There is a 10 year guarantee.

The price of the property, a finalising date, and any loans you may have applied for should also be detailed here.

### Inheritance of property
The inheritance law in France is far more restrictive than in the UK. If you are concerned about leaving your French property to someone it is a good idea to look at the different ways of purchasing property as there can be different implications depending on which method you choose. Do get professional legal advice before entering into any agreement.

## HELP WITH CONTRACTS

When you and the vendor of a property have reached an agreement, there will still be various matters to be cleared up before the Sale Contract can be established. Under French Law, two types of pre-contractual agreement are possible:

### Promesse de vente (unilateral agreement to sell)
The vendor agrees to sell you the property by a certain time, for a set price and according to certain conditions. This arrangement allows you some reflection time but you will be required to pay a deposit (approximately 10% of the full price) which you will lose on withdrawal.

### Compromis de vente
This type of contract is far more legally binding. Here, both you and the vendor are both immediately committed to the change in ownership of the property concerned. However, certain 'way out' clauses can be included in the agreement which are known as **conditions suspensives.** These clauses usually concern such matters as the granting of a mortgage, getting a **certificat d'urbanisme** (town planning report) etc. These clauses must be met or you are entitled to cancel the agreement and get your 10% deposit back.

### The Acte Authentique de Vente (conveyance)
As soon as the notaire (see section on **Notaires**) has all the necessary information, a **projet de l'acte** can be produced. This is a draft contract, a copy of which is sent to both you and the vendor to look over before signing.

The **Acte Authentique** itself will reiterate the clauses in the precontractual agreement as well as clarifying any more details. It is required to include the following:

- identification of both parties in the agreement;
- identification of the property in precise terms and the title to

the property, known as the **origine de propriété**;

- the **propriété de jouissance** which gives the date when you as the new owner will take possession of the property and will be entitled to use it;

- an **urbanisme** which restates any town planning regulations affecting the property as discovered by the notaire;

- any guarantees and estimates.

## HELP WITH TAXES

When setting up residence in France, there are several French taxes which you will be liable to pay.

### Government Registration Tax
This tax is payable when you are completing your purchase and, when added to the fees of the notaire, amounts to between 11% and 16% of the property's purchase price.

You will also be required to pay taxes which are the equivalent to UK Land Registry fees and Stamp Duty. The rate at which you will be taxed depends on the size of your property and its grounds; the type of buildings on the land; the age of the property. Properties less than three years old are exempt from Stamp Duty. Once you have bought property in France, you must register it with the tax authorities. If not actually living in France, you should contact the **Centre des Impôts des Non-résidents**. Your ownership should be registered with the tax authorities before April 30th of any year.

As an owner of French property, you will be liable to pay two types of local taxes which are equivalent to rates, the **taxe foncière** and **taxe d'habitation**.

### Taxe Foncière
This tax is levied by the commune in which your property is located, and is levied on you as proprietor. Your name will be added to a register at your local Mairie; this comprises lists of owners, tax rates paid and notional letting value of property concerned. New buildings—those less than two years old—as well as agricultural buildings are exempt from this tax.

### Taxe d'Habitation
This local tax is not necessarily payable by the owner of a property,

but by its occupant who may be a friend or relation of the owner for example. The rate of tax payable is determined by the building's amenities and size. The basic rate is calculated according to the nominal letting value of property in the local area with adjustments added on.

## Letting your property

Even if you do not actually live in France, you will have to pay French taxes when letting your property. Your tenants will pay 33.33% of the rent agreed in tax. You should make a return on your income from rent to the Centre des Impôts des Non-Résidents. As long as the French tax rate is no higher than that in the UK, you should be able to claim a rebate or offset the amount paid in tax against other Income Tax.

## Trusts

The French law on trusts is different from that in the UK; you cannot hold a property on trust for someone in the same way. Also, you cannot put your property into trust; there will be tax implications if you try to operate in France as you can do in the UK. It is therefore wise to get professional help or to read up on the subject of trusts thoroughly before embarking on any such arrangement.

## HELP WITH INSURANCE

You are required by French law to take out third party insurance as soon as you move into your accommodation or as soon as works have started on your future home. This is known as **Civil Propriétaire**.

It is also advisable to take out insurance against fire, theft, etc. Comprehensive policies known as **assurances multirisque** are available, as are specific policies. The sum insured should reflect your insurable interest or potential loss according to the contract arranged. Some British companies are already able to offer cover for properties in France, a practice which should be more commonly available after 1992.

- If you are a co-owner (see **Different sorts of accommodation**), the building itself and all communal areas should already be covered. You should also take out insurance on your own belongings.

- If you are having a property built, you are responsible for insurance as soon as the work starts.

- If you are letting your property, it is the responsibility of your tenant(s) to take out insurance, at least against fire, on your behalf.

## THE PROFESSIONALS

At some point during the purchase of a property in France you are likely to need the services of a professional person from one field or another.

### Le Notaire (notary)

Every property transaction must be overseen by a notaire according to French law. Le notaire is a representative of Public Authority and is controlled by the Ministry of Justice and the Chambre des Notaires. A notaire must be impartial between the two parties of a sale and is responsible for legally validating the deeds involved, advising clients and for drawing up the necessary contracts.

In the provinces, you may encounter **Notaires de Familles** (or **Conseils de Familles** as trustees). Such professionals act as tax consultants (as well as in the usual property transactions).

When working as a sale negotiator, the notaire is entitled to a legally determined sum as commission. This is usually payable by you as purchaser rather than the vendor. A notaire can act as an estate agent when a group of co-owners want to sell their property. When acting as intermediaries between sale parties, a notaire has the following responsibilities:

- verification of the identity of the vendor and his/her right to sell;

- obtaining the relevant Land Registry papers (showing any planning objections to the property);

- contacting anyone with pre-emption rights to the property (determining whether they plan to use such rights);

- contacting the **Conservation des Hypothèques** (mortgage/Land Registry) which will issue an **état hors formalité**. This shows any mortgages, securities etc on the property. Such debts must be payable and lower than the sale price to avoid redemption proceedings.

Paying for your property through a notaire will give you protection. S/he can withhold payment if it is revealed that the vendor has used the property as collateral on a loan until a **negative état sur formalité** has been obtained.

When buying a property, you will have to pay what is known as **frais de notaire** comprising the notaire's fees (including money paid on your behalf), taxes, dues plus various contingency duties. Fees can be **émoluements d'actes (simple)** or **émoluements de négotiation** and follow a set scale.

- Costs are high overall but vary between regions and with different types and values of property.

- The notaire retains the original of the contract, giving you and the vendor copies known as **l'expéditions.**

- Once you have registered the sale at the **Bureau des Hypothèques,** no one else has any claim over the building.

- The relevant section of the Title Deed is sent to the Land Registry.

## The Estate Agent

In France, 50% of all property transactions are dealt with by estate agents; the remainder are arranged privately or by notaires. The professional estate agent must have the following:

- Professional competence (as demonstrated by a diploma or length of experience).

- Financial guarantees (to cover all money dealt with above FF500,000).

- Professional indemnity insurance.

- A valid professional permit covering **transactions sur immeubles et fonds de commerce** (real estate and business transactions) issued by the préfecture (headquarters) of police.

NB. The estate agent must not be banned from or incapable of practising the profession.

An estate agent will give you advice as your representative and concerning market values etc involved in property transaction. Negotiations cannot be initiated unless the estate agent holds a **Mandat de Vente** (a written power of attorney for sale) from the vendor, or a **Mandat de Recherche** (a power of attorney to make a search) from you as the purchaser. The vendor will usually have to pay the estate agent's commission, the amount of which is covered by a power of attorney, on written completion of the transaction.

- Estate agents can fix the amount of commission they receive, but their scale of charges must be on open display.

- The commission represents a percentage of the purchase price.

- Estate agents are not permitted to charge for anything not referred to in the power of attorney.

The sale itself usually progresses as follows:

- You as potential buyer make an initial unilateral promise to purchase. This is passed on by the estate agent together with a sum as specified in the power of attorney issued by you.

- When an agreement has been reached—the initial offer usually being accepted—the sale goes ahead with the signing of a **Compromis de Vente** (see **Help with contracts**) at the office either of the notaire or estate agent.

NB. The Acte Authentique must be signed in the presence of a notaire.

An estate agent may also be involved when letting property. In this case, the estate agent must be issued with a written power of attorney either by you, the landlord/lady, or by your prospective tenant. The estate agent will be entitled to fees payable (in equal parts) by you and the future tenant(s). The estate agent will be paid as a negotiator in the transaction, but may also charge extra, eg for drawing up a lease and inventory.

### Surveying your property
In France, having a structural survey done is not common practice as it is in the UK. This is because stringent construction and building regulations mean that there is usually no need.

- The vendor or the building company working on a property are obliged to issue guarantees on the property (see **Renovating older properties**, page 80).

- The builder must be insured for each work undertaken (lasting 10 years and covering default in case of bankruptcy).

Ask your notaire to include details of any guarantees on the property and a list of builders involved in your agreement.

If you decide that you do want a survey carried out on your future property, you can employ an **expert géomètre** (building contractor) to do it. A notaire or estate agent can carry out a simple survey if required.

## FINANCING YOUR PURCHASE

If you need to borrow money to buy your house or flat in France, you have two choices, with some variations. You can either borrow in the UK with UK security, or borrow in France with French security.

### Borrowing in the UK
If approaching your own bank, you may be offered the following:

- A loan facility with a first or second mortgage on your home as security or using other assets.

- An advance in addition to an already established UK mortgage, gained through a specialist mortgage loan company.

- A loan using your UK home as security.

Such facilities should be available through all banks and building societies, though fees charged and lending policies may vary.

It may also be possible to obtain a foreign currency loan (in F Francs) from your bank with your property in the UK as security. However, an element of curency risk is involved in this sort of arrangement. This means that if the bank had to sell your French property because you defaulted on payments, money could be lost in currency exchange. An additional security margin will therefore be required to safeguard against such an eventuality.

Additional life insurance cover may also be required by the lending company as well as guarantees. Methods of repayment should be discussed with your bank or building society.

### Borrowing in France
Sources of real estate loans are varied and include banks, financial institutions, **caisses d'épargne** (savings banks) and notaires. It is however most common to obtain assistance from high street banks and specialist institutions who usually provide long term finance for the buying of property. Such organisations will have well established schemes covering such transactions.

- Repayment loans are available to cover between 70% and 80% of the purchase price or cost of construction of your property. Repayment can be arranged over a period of between 2 and 20 years, in quarterly or monthly instalments. These will usually be paid through a French account and will incorporate premiums for life and disablement insurance policies. A mortgage on your French property will provide security.

- You can buy a property in France before the sale of your UK home is completed, with the aid of a bridging loan. This will usually have to be repaid within two years unless the sale of your property goes through before this time when repayment must be made immediately. Approximately 70% of the estimated value of the property you are selling will be covered by the loan. Interest will either be taken monthly from your account or along with the capital. Security—as above.

- Currency loans involve borrowing money in a currency of your choice. This type of arrangement can be complicated since there are no fixed rates and an extra security margin will be taken.

Since organisations offer various terms and conditions for lending, it is a good idea to shop around before making your choice. Be particularly careful to compare like with like, eg ensure that the overall price of each policy includes the same benefits and fees.

Both residents and non-residents can apply for loans with favourable interest rates for the purchase of property in France which is to be used as a main residence. Such loans, however, are not usually available to foreigners though an **épargne logement** loan (a savings plan for buying a home) may be applied for.

At the present time there are no endowment or pension scheme mortgages in France. A mortgage is discharged if you sell your property so that a new one has to be arranged on any new accommodation you buy; a penalty ('early repayment' fee) may be charged by your lending bank.

A French bank will calculate the amount of money available for a mortgage according to your cash flow. A mortgage should be granted as long as your outgoings plus your mortgage repayments equal less than 30% of your pre-tax income.

### Help with language problems

Some French banks in London as well as some British banks in France have specialist departments to help you if you do not speak French.

## MAKING MONEY FROM YOUR PROPERTY

Many British people are buying property in France with a view to converting it to a 'bed & breakfast', guest house, or **gîte** (home).

### Bed & breakfast
No prior authorisation is required to open a bed & breakfast, though you must register your property with the **Registre du Commerce** as a commercial entity.

### Guest houses
French **pensions de famille** are similar to guest houses providing lodging, breakfast and evening meal to their guests. As before, authorisation is not necessary, but registration is. If you want alcohol to be available on your premises you must get a licence from your local Town Hall or Préfecture.

### Gîtes
These are usually quite basic and offer cheap accommodation. The National Organisation of French Gîtes can authorise you to use the term **Gîtes Rureaux** (rural gîtes). You must offer your property for rent for at least three months a year and you must live close by. The areas of the property which are used commercially and those which are lived in will be specified in the sale deed. Less tax is payable on a gîte than on either a bed & breakfast or a guest house and other tax incentives may be available.

### Formalities
The purchase of any of the above is much the same as buying a residential property. You must however inform your notaire that you intend to convert your property before the drafting of any formal documents. When the **Acte de Vente** has been drawn up, you must inform the Registre du Commerce of your conversion. From this point onwards you will be responsible for any taxation connected with the change in usage of the property. If you do not pay such taxes, you will incur the following penalties:

- payment of Stamp Duty at 11.20% of the purchase price;
- payment of a penalty at 8% of the above;
- payment of VAT on any profits you make from your venture.

### Buying a farm
The French government may grant financial aid to a young person

(under 35) or to someone who holds a Diploma recognised by the French Ministry of Agriculture. If you hold a Diploma which has no French equivalent, you should contact the Ministry. You may then be granted an equivalent qualification depending on your educational background.

The **Plan de Développement** may also assist you with farm modernisation and in less popular geographical areas. Entry into this scheme requires that you:

- practise farming as your main occupation;

- are sufficiently qualified or have enough experience as a young farmer;

- are able to keep simple accounts on your farm.

When buying a farm in France it is important to consider whether you wish to remain a British citizen. If this is the case, you must write a formal declaration for the Treasury at the French Finance Ministry confirming this intention.

### Letting your property

NB. Please refer to sections on Taxation, Insurance and Estate Agents.

There are several ways of finding people to rent your property. The following guidelines may be helpful.

- Advertise in UK newspapers. You will then have the best opportunity to 'vet' prospective tenants personally though unless living in France yourself overseeing any arrangements made could be difficult.

- Pay a French agent to deal with the letting of your property. Some agents may also manage rented accommodation for their owners. Commission charged is usually between 10% and 15%.

- You can contact international agencies which deal with rented accommodation all round the world.

- A letting service is sometimes offered by the management of blocks of flats. Look at the way a block is maintained as a guide to how good a service you are likely to get.

- Some individuals or small organisations exist who will manage your property in your absence. Your bank in France may be able to help you find such managers. You should issue your tenant(s) with a Letting Contract covering the following:

- a description of the premises;

- the letting period;

- specification of communal areas and those for exclusive use by tenant(s);

- amount of rent charged and terms of payment (excluding charges);

- the amount of deposit required (not more than the equivalent of two months rent).

For more details on letting out your property in France, contact your local library.

## RENTING ACCOMMODATION

The most common type of rented accommodation in France is a block of flats known as an **Immeuble**. It is also possible to rent a house, though this is more common in the suburbs than in urban areas. A fairly good quality house with a garden here will cost about the same in rent as a Paris flat. The further away from large conurbations you go, the cheaper rents should be.

It is hard to find good rented accommodation in the provinces, except in some of the larger towns and cities. These can be very expensive however, the prices in Lyon, Grenoble, Nice and Cannes being comparable with those of Paris. Other cities such Strasbourg, Toulouse, and Marseille tend to have more reasonably priced accommodation.

Many flats are pre-World War One and are in blocks serviced by a **concierge**. They are usually arranged as a number of smallish rooms opening off a single corridor. Such flats can be rather claustrophobic and dark. More modern buildings however are generally more welcoming with larger, lighter rooms and sometimes an underground garage.

Some blocks are purpose-built for letting; others are owned and let by private landlords/ladies who use the services of agents who (as mentioned in the previous section) may manage flats and houses. The service offered by these agencies varies widely and is something to be borne in mind when looking for rented accommodation.

### Unfurnished rentals
When the French say 'unfurnished', this is exactly what they mean.

You may easily find no light fixtures, kitchen cabinets, stove, refrigerator, medicine cabinet—perhaps even no kitchen sink. Ask for details. Furniture, cabinets, shelving, bedding and blankets can all be rented but at quite high rates.

## Legal aspects of renting accommodation

The **Loi Méhaignerie** governs the letting of accommodation in France though reference may sometimes be made to the previous **Loi Quillot**. Perhaps you are planning to move to France but want to look around before buying a property. If so, a holiday let may be a good idea. Holiday letting is not covered by the Loi Méhaignerie.

## The lease

You *must* have a lease, preferably along the following lines:

- A full description of the premises being rented; its permitted users; an inventory of all fixtures and fittings (for communal and exclusive use); when the lease is to commence; the amount of rent payable with frequency of payment; any review provisions.

- If there is a rent review clause, it can only be exercised once a year. Rent revision is linked to the Cost of Construction Index. You may need to ask for receipts for the rent you pay as these are not required by law.

- Your landlord/lady cannot require you to pay the rent by direct debit while promissory notes on your part are not permissible. You may be required to pay a deposit of not more than the equivalent of two months rent which must be returned to you within two months of the end of your lease (less any rent owed).

- You will probably have to pay a large proportion of the landlord/lady's service charges and local rates (see section of Taxation). A small tax on leasing (**droit de bail**) will also be payable.

- There are some provisions which are illegal and unenforceable. For example, you cannot be required to take out insurance with a particular company.

- If you are going to be living in a building owned **en copropriété** (see **Outright purchase**, page 80), you must be given certain details of the Règlement de Copropriété.

- The costs associated with organising a lease are to be shared equally between you and your landlord/lady.

- You must respect any user clauses in the lease and take responsibility for 'tenants repairs' (ie those not associated with structural problems, accidents from outside etc). Exercise commonsense regarding your behaviour in the rented accommodation and the relationship between you and its owner is more likely to run smoothly.

- Your landlord/lady has responsibility for maintaining the premises to a standard appropriate to their intended usage.

- Your lease is unassignable without the consent of your landlord/lady.

- Consent is also required if you should wish to sub-let your accommodation. You may also be required to disclose the amount of rent you are charging. The Loi Méhaignerie does not cover the sub-letting of accommodation.

### Repairs to rented accommodation

This is an area notorious for confusion and friction between tenants and landlords/ladies. If asked about such arrangements, a landlord/lady might tell you to contact the copropriété of your building; *you should not agree to this*, persevere with him/her. Also, do not claim against your insurance if at all possible. It can be a good idea to call in a **huissier** (someone who acts as a bailiff and process server) to make reports on accidents etc. Such reports are considered incontrovertible by the courts and can not only prevent a landlord/lady denying responsibility for repairs but may actually spur them into action!

### The Loi Méhaignerie

Both you and your landlord/lady have certain rights under this law.

- Any lease granted must be for a definite period of at least three years. During this time, possession cannot be reclaimed except under conditions specified in the lease.

- The one exception to these rules occurs if the lease has a provision allowing repossession for 'unprofessional' or 'family' reasons.

- At the end of the three year letting term your landlord/lady takes possession of the accommodation or the lease is renewed for another three years. If the latter is the case, a notice detailing new terms should be issued to you at least six months prior to the expiration of your lease. If you find the new terms acceptable, you should confirm this at least three months before the end of the lease period or you may be deemed as having accepted a notice to quit.

- If you wish to leave your accommodation, you may do so at any time with three months notice unless you have lost or changed your job in which case the notice required is one month.

- If neither you nor your landlord/lady do anything within the time limits specified, the original lease is renewed and its terms stand.

## MORE INFORMATION ON HOUSE-HUNTING

*La Centrale des Particuliers*
35 avenue de Villiers
75854 Paris Cedex 17 (tel: 47 66 52 56)
Magazine published by a non-profit organisation; it lists property and other items for sale or rent.

*De Particulier à Particulier*
8 rue Général Delestraint
75016 Paris
Publication with private (non-agent) ads for accommodation.

**Centre de Documentation et d'Information de l'Assurance**
3 bis rue de la Chaussée d'Antin
70559 Paris (tel: 48 24 96 12 or 47 70 89 39)
For information on insurance.

**Agences immobilières** (estate agents)
See Yellow Pages. Also listed under **Agences de Location et de Propriétés**.

## HOUSEHOLD SERVICES

### Maintenance and other expenses
Not only are you expected to pay for heat and utilities when you rent but for many other costs as well. Repairs in France are often the tenant's responsibility, not the landlord's; the lift, night watchman,

and rubbish disposal may cost extra too. In addition to one- to three-months rent as a guarantee deposit you may need to pay advance rent for several additional months. Sometimes you have to buy or rent existing fixtures. This often adds up to considerable initial expense, so be prepared.

Tenants are charged for any item that is damaged, so a careful pre-entry inventory (**état des lieux**) is **imperative**. Note all the pre-existent cracks, leaks and damages (inside and out), or you may have to pay for them when you leave.

Plumbing is usually adequate although it may not always meet everyone's standards. The hot water heater (gas or electric) is often located in the bathroom.

By law all chimneys in use must be cleaned annually. Look in the phone book for **fumisterie** and be sure to keep your bill as proof—to keep your home insurance valid.

Rubbish removal and other service charges should be covered in any lease you sign as the renter of an apartment or a house. There is also a yearly tax assessment on your TV.

## Gas and Electricity

By some standards it costs a great deal of money to live in France. More flats and houses—even the newer ones—have limited facilities for heating. Central heating is controlled by the date not the temperature, being turned on in October, off in April. Some foreign residents, therefore supplement central heating with portable electric heaters.

Gas and electricity bills usually arrive every four months and can be paid at the post office using a form (**mandat**) or by post. A notice from the meter reader will be sent to you so that you can be home on the day it is to be read, or you can arrange to give the key to the concierge. For emergency repairs (electricity, plumbing, heat) phone 47 07 99 99.

The domestic electricity supply is usually 220v AC, 50 cycles, although 110v, 115v and 127v are still supplied to some areas. Plug fittings for smaller appliances are usually the standard European size with two pins while larger appliances are often fitted with three-pin plugs.

Although there is mains gas, great use is made of bottled gas in France. This is probably because the electricity supply tends to be prone to failure from time to time so that back-up source of fuel can be a good idea.

## Water

Water is charged for by a local **Cie des Eaux de...** (name of town) rather than by your local authority. The amount you are charged depends on the actual amount actually used by your household as measured by a meter.

## DOMESTIC HELP

Since there are many rules regarding employment and since rates of pay change from time to time, it is wise to get information from an employment bureau. Help is hard to find, very expensive, and highly taxed. Domestic help can be sought through friends, local shopkeepers, other foreign nationals, and friends or relatives of your friends, that is, by word of mouth. Some people have luck through English newspapers, but in general try to avoid newspaper ads and agencies. Your concierge may be a resource, but remember, if you hire the concierge's cousin or niece (or whatever), problems may develop with the concierge if you ever want to fire that person.

Most people settle for part-time help. **Femmes de ménage** are cleaning women; **bonnes à tout faire** are general maids. Much of the available help is Spanish, Portuguese or North African, and you can often find them through their own churches. You can also register with your local branch of the National Employment Agency (**Agence Locale pour l'Emploi**).

### Social Security

All help—full- or part-time—must be covered by social security. You register with 'Union pour Recouvrement des Cotisations de Sécurité Sociale et d'Allocations Familiales' (called URSSAF for short). You will receive an S/S number valid for all employees you hire. In Paris the office is at 27 avenue du Général Leclerc, BP 51, 77001 Melun Cedex; tel: 44 39 92 54.

If you hire someone without social security, you are obligated to submit a declaration on him/her *within a week* to Caisse Primaire Central de Sécurité Sociale, 69 bis rue de Dunkerque, 75019 Paris.

There is a great deal of paperwork involved with employing help. At any stationery store you can get a **carnet de bulletin de paie ou de salaire** (payroll or salary register) in which to keep the complex records. The town hall (**mairie**) of your district (**arrondissement**) can give you further information.

## Au Pairs

Few French domestic employees speak English. Therefore, many families—especially those with young children—get an **au pair**, meaning a student from another country (usually young women who are in France to learn the language). An **au pair** is 'one of the family', and does a few hours of light work (usually taking care of children) a day in exchange for room and board and some pocket money. In France they are often Dutch, Scandinavian, or German. There are special bureaux that handle **au pairs**; they will tell you the tax arrangements. If your **au pair** comes from outside France, it is your responsibility to be sure she has a residence permit, worker permit, and social security card.

## Baby sitters

Sources of baby sitters by the hour include:

- Bureau de Placement des Etudiants: 13 rue du Four, 75006 Paris;
- Medical Students: 26 rue St Jacques, 75104 Paris;
- Institut Catholique: 21 rue d'Assas, 75006 Paris;
- Operation Biberon (baby bottle); tel: 45 86 19 44. Medical students from the University of Paris will also tutor, translate, and give nursing care.

## Settling in

Once you and your family are established in your new home in France there will be much to get used to, some of which won't seem too strange and some which might seem very alien. The standard French working day begins early, usually about 8 o'clock in the morning but never later than 9. There has traditionally been a 2 or 3 hour break for lunch starting at noon or 1300 hours (it is usual to use the 24 hour clock in France). The working day ends between 1800 and 1930 hours.

## SHOPPING

Before doing your shopping in France, it is a good idea to familiarise yourself with the money you will be using to pay for it. One UK pound is approximately equivalent to 9.81 French Francs (FF). Get a selection of French money (eg from a bank) before leaving home so that you and your family can all get used to handling it. Notes and coins exist in the following denominations:

Notes: 50, 100 and 500 FF
Coins: 1, 2, 5, 20, 50 centimes; 1, 2, 5, and 10 FF

There are 100 centimes to the franc. The relatively new copper 10 franc piece is similar to the much less valuable 20 centime piece, so be careful not to confuse them. Currency exchange offices are located in airports, air terminals, railway stations and most banks. **American Express** also operates this service: 11 rue Scribe, 75009 Paris, tel: 42 66 09 09. Offices are open from 9 to 1700 hours, Monday to Friday and from 9 to noon on Saturdays.

Although department stores, supermarkets and many other shops are open all day, small shops tend to close at noon for some 3 or 4 hours and close in the evening at 1900 hours.

You will have the best of two worlds for food shopping in France; the huge, efficient, relatively inexpensive and well stocked super-markets and the colourful street markets and local shops. Food shops are often open on Sundays and closed all day on Mondays. You may find that bags are not provided for taking shopping home from small shops, or that they are very weak so that it is a good idea to take your own. The names for particular types of smaller shops are as follows:

- **la boulangerie**, the bakery shop
- **la boucherie**, the butchers
- **l'épicerie**, the grocer's shop
- **la crèmerie**, the dairy produce shop
- **la charcuterie**, the pork shop

Department stores are good places to shop. They have a wide range of goods and offer an opportunity to compare prices. They often have English-speaking guides as well. The best known chain stores are *Le Printemps*, *Au Bon Marché*, *Trois Quartiers* and *Samaritaine*. Sales are usually in January and during the last weeks of June and July.

There are now shopping precincts and discount shops on the outskirts of many French towns and cities. In city centres, particularly in the provinces, a new look has recently been given to commercial areas by creating **rues piétonnes** (streets for pedestrians) which are lined with shops. Benches, fountains and shrubbery create a pleasant atmosphere.

*NB* If you normally reside outside the EC and are in France for a stay of less than 6 months, you can benefit from deduction of the TVA (value added tax) on goods bought in France. Purchase has to be a minimum of FF 800 from a single shop. At the border, when leaving the country, give the **bordereau rosé** (the pink document you will have received from the shop) to the customs officials. The deduction will be forwarded to you.

## FOOD AND DRINK

The French prefer to have their main meal—**le déjeuner**—at midday and a lighter meal—**le dîner**—in the evening. **Souper** is a very late evening meal. The old habit of having a very long lunch break is dying out and being reduced to around 30 minutes. Fast-food is being reluctantly accepted by the French.

Contrary to what many foreigners might think, everyday home cooking in France is quite simple and becoming more so with increased usage of the microwave, **micro ondes**. When entertaining, however, dishes can be very elaborate. Some very popular French dishes are as follows:

- **Coquilles St Jacques**: scallops served with parsley butter and cream sauce;

- **Cassoulet**: kidney bean stew prepared with pork and mutton;

- **Bouillabaisse**: fish soup with saffron;

- **Quenelles**: finger-shaped, seasoned dumplings made with various forcemeats, usually cooked in fish sauce;

- **Tripes à la mode de Caen**: tripe cooked in apple cider;

- **Coq au vin**: chicken cooked in red wine sauce.

### Beverages

In addition to strong coffee, often with lots of sugar, brandy and wine are the most popular drinks in France. **Apéritif** wines are usually acceptable before a meal: or if entertaining, try **kir**, a little crème de cassis mixed into chilled white wine. For brandy and water, a favourite drink, ask for **fine à l'eau**. Beer is also fairly popular, especially Dutch and German varieties.

A recent study of French food and wine customs reported that during the last 10 years, wine consumption in France has dropped by 15% with 20% of young people abstaining from alcohol. The use of mineral water, on the other hand, has doubled. The wines of France fall into 4 categories:

- AOC (**Appelation Origine Contrôlée**) or 'controlled place of origin'; encompasses 16% of France's total production and including the best wines.

- VDQS (**Vins délimités de Qualité Supérieure**); a classification of good French wines, slightly under AOC.

- **Vins de Pays**; country wines.

- **Vins de table** (table wines); everyday French wines representing almost 70% of production.

The main wine regions of France are Bordeaux, Loire, Alsace, Burgundy and Côtes du Rhône. Always store wine horizontally so that the cork is kept wet and no air can enter and spoil the wine.

## CONVERSIONS

### Metric system
The following conversions may be useful:

| | |
|---|---|
| 1 mile | 1.6 kilometres; 1 kilometre = 5/8 mile; to convert kilometres to miles, multiply by 0.62. |
| 1 yard | 0.914 metres; 1 inch = 2.54 centimetres; 1 metre = 39.37 inches, 3.28 feet or 1.09 yards |
| 1 acre | 0.405 hectares; 1 hectare = 2.47 acres |
| 1 ounce | 28.35 grams; 1 gram = 0.035 ounce |
| 1 pound | 453.39 grams; 1 kilogram = 2.2 pounds |
| 1 pint | 0.473 litres; 1 litre = 33.815 ounces; 1 litre = 1.06 liquid quarts or 0.908 dry quarts |
| 1 metric (long) ton | 2240 pounds |

### Temperatures
To convert Celsius to Fahrenheit, just multiply the centigrade temperature by 1.8 and then add 32. To convert Fahrenheit to Celsius, subtract 32 from the Fahrenheit temperature, multiply by 5 and divide by 9.

### Cooking measures
Meat in France is sold by the kilo (1 kilo equals 2.2 pounds). Some useful phrases when purchasing meat are:

| | |
|---|---|
| *un kilo* | one kilo |
| *une livre* | half a kilo |
| *une demi-livre* | half a livre |
| *un morceau* | a piece |
| *une tranche* | a slice |
| *épais* | thick |
| *mince* | thin |
| *la moitié* | half |

Should you have a European cookbook and want to try some of the recipes, the following terms for meat may be useful.

**Boeuf—beef**
*côte première*—prime rib
*entrecôte*—sirloin
*faux filet*—tenderloin
*rumpsteak*—sirloin chop
*tranche carrée*—bottom
  round-swiss steak
*pièce ronde*—eye round
*jarret*—leg
*flanchet*—flank
*grumbeau*—brisket
*plat de côtes*—ribs
*beefsteak*—steak

**Jambon—pork**
*épaule*—shoulder
*côte première*—loin chops
*filet*—loin
*jarret*—hocks
*jambon*—ham
*costines*—spare ribs
*lard fumé*—bacon

**Mouton—mutton;**
**Agneau—lamb**
*épaule*—shoulder
*côtelette*—chops
*filet*—loin
*poitrine*—breast

# 7
# Health and Welfare

## THE FRENCH NATIONAL HEALTH SERVICE OR SECURITE SOCIALE

If you are living and working in France, you are obliged to join the **Sécurité Sociale**. Both you and your employer must make regular contributions to ensure that you and your dependants are always adequately covered. If you are self-employed, you pay a percentage of your taxable income as your contribution which will then be deductable for Income Tax purposes. If you are resident in France but not employed, you can make voluntary contributions to the scheme. If you are retired (in the sense that you are entitled to a State Pension at 'home'), you and your spouse are automatically entitled to health benefits under the Sécurité Sociale free of any contribution. In this last case, take the form E121 to the Sécurité Sociale office as it will prove your entitlement to your pension.

When joining the French Health Service, make an initial visit to the **Relations Internationales** Department of Sécurité Sociale where you should be able to get some help and advice.

- If both you and your spouse are registering with the Health Service, take a marriage certificate *plus* an official translation with you. You may well be told that it was not necessary to have this done, but if you turn up without a translation it is likely you will be sent away to get one done!

- If you are thinking of making voluntary contributions to the Sécurité Sociale, it may be best to think again. The contributions you will be making may well be quite expensive and a cheaper option is to take out private medical insurance in the UK or ensure that any policy already held will cover you on a permanent basis.

## Health care

The Sécurité Sociale works by reimbursing you for the amount of the charges you incur which are covered by the scheme. You can choose your own doctor or clinic (look under *Professions*—Yellow Pages—or ask neighbours or workmates for recommendations) and pay them directly, applying for reimbursement afterwards. Some hospitals, doctors etc can be used completely free of charge while others will be only partially covered by the Sécurité Sociale, the proportion of the cost paid being previously arranged and publicised. Reimbursement will vary between 70% and 80% of the authorised scale of charges according to a number of factors. Contact the Sécurité Sociale for information and help with the system as it can get very complicated and confusing.

Every large town has at least one **hôpital conventioné** which provides services free of charge, as well as doctors and other medical services. These services, however, can often be rather limited. The hôpitaux conventionés have no completely private rooms, for instance.

The Sécurité Sociale will reimburse you for your medical charges on the basis of a **feuille de soins**, a form which acts as a receipt for any payment for medical services you have made. This is usually completed by a doctor or chemist and must be lodged with your local **Caisse Primaire**.

## Health insurance

Since only a proportion of your medical charges will be reimbursed by the Sécurité Sociale, you will need to be able to cope with the difference. This is done using the **mutuelle**, the French private health insurance. In many occupations, it is obligatory to join the scheme and almost every profession and trade has its own mutuelle. Such a plan will cover not only the difference between the amount you can claim back from the Health Service and what your treatment actually cost, but also 'tops up' your retirement pension. You can pay for private medical services using mutuelles and there are also Private Health Insurance Policies issued by insurance companies. Certificate E111 (Department of Social Security) will give you limited medical entitlements but it is generally better to have your own medical insurance cover.

When dealing with the Sécurité Sociale there are two basic things to remember:

- Try to find out in advance what you are entitled to under the system. If your treatment is not too urgent, find out what the final cost will be at your chosen clinic. The chances are that equivalent services will be available at several institutions and the proportion of costs not covered by the Sécurité Sociale will vary.

• Keep a copy of all feuilles de soins sent. Either take them personally to the Sécurité Sociale or send the forms by registered post.

### Services for English-speaking patients

Quite a few French doctors speak English but unless you are reasonably fluent in French and familiar with medical terms in the language, you could run into difficulties, especially if the illness in question is serious. However, help is at hand:

• **British Consulates** have lists of English-speaking doctors, though bear in mind that these offices are only open for relatively short hours each day.

• The **International Association for Medical Assistance to Travellers** (IAMAT) provides English-speaking medical practitioners who work for the organisation and charge fixed fees for their services. Head Office: 417 Center Street, Lewistone, New York NY 14092, USA.

• **SOS** is a service providing medical aid and, if necessary, repatriation (emergency number: 93 08 66 10).

• **The AA** has set up AA St John Alert, an emergency service for travellers. There is an emergency contact number and advice is available on a whole range of medical matters. For further information contact: AA St John Alert, Fanum House, Basingstoke, Hants RG21 2BR.

If you have no health insurance and no money, there are several associations offering free consultations and health care given by volunteer doctors and nurses.

• At the Red Cross in Paris, the **REMEDE Association** offers free consultations. The address is: 33 rue de la Folie-Régnault, 75011 Paris.

• The SMIG (**Service Médical Itinérant Gratuit**) van provides health care in certain areas: Bastille (Monday, 2-5pm); Motte-Picquet (Tuesday, 10am); Gare de Lyon (Wednesday, 9am-12 noon); Gare du Nord (Friday, 2-5pm); Gare d'Austerlitz (Thursday, 2-5 pm); Place d'Italie (Sunday, 8.30am-12 noon).

## Prescriptions

If you have a repeat prescription in the UK, find out whether the medication is available in France and if so under what brand name through your doctor or an International Pharmacy. French pharmacists will not necessarily be familiar with non-French brand names and may not accept foreign prescriptions. It may be difficult to obtain exact equivalents of some drugs (notably certain anticoagulants and heart pills). If you require such medication, get your doctor to give you a long-term prescription or import them personally, preferably in their original, sealed packaging and clearly marked for Customs. Some imported pharmaceutical products are available in Paris at these addresses:

- 135 Champs Elysées, Paris;
- Pharmacie Anglo-Américaine, 37 avenue Marceau, 75008 Paris (a British/American pharmacy for those whose French isn't too good).

Lists of chemists in your area which are open at night or at weekends should be available at all chemists. If you are covered by the Sécurité Sociale, apply for reimbursement of prescription charges as you will not get them automatically.

## DENTAL & EYE CARE

Neither of these should present any problems for you though if you have any major dental work which needs doing, it might be wise to get it done before leaving home by your own dentist, especially if your French is not fluent. Once in France, recommendations by friends or colleagues are a good way to find good dentists and opticians. Many foreign residents have been impressed with the new 'Dial-a Dentist' services for emergency home treatment, that care for housebound patients and provide care for those staying in temporary accommodation (hotels etc). Dentists in radio cars respond quickly to calls anywhere in Paris and carry portable equipment; some speak English. Phone 47 37 51 00 for dental emergencies (**SOS Dentaire**).

## IMMUNISATION

It is a good idea to be immunised against tetanus, typhoid, typhus, polio and diphtheria. These immunisations are not strictly required, but are always worth having if you are planning to travel. There is a lot of travel between France and Africa where cholera is still found. It might, therefore, be a good idea to add this to your list of precautionary immunisations.

## SEXUAL MATTERS

There are many organisations providing help, advice and counselling on contraception, unwanted pregnancy and sexually transmitted diseases. Family planning and information centres do not provide medical services, but hospitals and clinics do provide information and counselling along with health care. To find out where to go, contact the following organisations:

- **Mouvement Français du Planning Familial**, 4 square Saint-Irénée, 75011 Paris;

- **Centre National d'Information sur les droits des Femmes**, (Women's rights) 7 rue du Jura, 75013 Paris;

- **Ligue Nationale contre les maladies vénériennes**, Institute Alfred-Fournier, 25 bd Saint-Jaques, 7566680 Paris.

(For the last type of problem, ie venereal disease, you can also go to your nearest hospital.)

## AIDS

There are a number of associations offering advice and information on AIDS (SIDA in French):

- AIDES, BP 759, 75123 Paris. Tel: 42 72 19 99.
- Vaincre le SIDA, BP 435, 75233 Paris.

Staff at the above organisations should be able to deal with any worries you may have and put you in touch with local associations all over France.

## ILLEGAL SUBSTANCES

If you need help with a drug-related problem contact the following organisations:

- **Centre médical Marmottan**, 17-19 rue d'Armaillé, 75017 Paris;

- **L'Abbaye**, 33 rue Linné, 75005 Paris (Tel: 47 07 57 37).

# 8
# Education

## THE FRENCH EDUCATIONAL SYSTEM

If you are thinking of enrolling your children in a French school (or even if you are not), it is important to know something about the French educational system. Besides, schools and universities are always a good topic of conversation.

As mentioned in chapter 1, the French have an excellent and highly competitive educational system, which is entirely free of charge from kindergarten right through to PhD level.

A French child starts secondary school after age eleven. There may be an entrance test which the expatriate child of that age must take to be admitted. Because of the differences in the age for starting school and in the curriculum, an expatriate child may be accepted at a lower grade (or perhaps higher) than would be the case in a school at home.

The grades in France start with the twelfth and end with the first, followed by **classe terminale**, which is the last year of high school. Thereafter, most students will take the **Baccalauréat**, but not everyone succeeds. The Baccalauréat (often called the 'Bac') is a very selective examination, without which entrance to a university is not possible.

The academic year starts in mid-September and ends in late June. Holidays consist of a few days for All Saints' Day, two weeks for Christmas, a week in February, and two weeks for Easter. In state schools Wednesday and Saturday afternoons are free. Many of the private schools have adopted a five-day, full-time schedule. Children go to school three hours in the morning and three hours in the afternoon. At the secondary level, class hours per week can reach thirty-five.

### Outline of the French educational structure

**Ecole Maternelle**
Up to 6 years old          Physical and sensory exercises and exercises
                           in language and observation

109

**Elementary School**

Preparatory (11ème)　Beginning reading, writing, spelling and
　　　　　　　　　　reasoning
Elementary I (10ème) Beginning history, geography, science by
　　　　　　　　　　observation, and grammar
Elementary II (9ème)
Intermediate I (8ème)
Intermediate II(7ème)

**Secondary School or Terminal Cycle** (11-16); Terminal cycle includes
continuation of elementary education with stress on vocational and
practical studies.

**Secondary: First or Observation Cycle**

6ème　　　　　Beginning foreign language
5ème　　　　　Beginning geometry, Latin, and algebra
4ème　　　　　Beginning second foreign language, Greek for
　　　　　　　students oriented towards Classique. A
3ème

**Secondary: Second Cycle or short secondary education (15 to 17 years
of age)**

Seconde　　　Beginning third foreign language for those
　　　　　　　students studying neither maths nor Latin
Première　　　Leading to the 'Bac' (seven main sections:
　　　　　　　philosophy, mathematical science, mathematics
　　　　　　　and technology, economics and humanities)
Classe Terminale

## SCHOOL POSSIBILITIES FOR FOREIGNERS

You can send your children to private English schools, bilingual
schools or French schools. All schools, particularly the outstanding
ones, are crowded and requirements are stiff, so you need to start
thinking about schools as soon as you know your assignment, well
ahead of arrival if possible.

### Private English-speaking schools

* **American School of Paris**, 41 rue Pasteur, 92210 St Cloud; tel: 46
02 54 43. The American School of Paris is in the western suburb of
St Cloud, about seven miles from the place de l'Etoile. There is a
bus service from Paris and most surrounding areas. Founded in
1946, the school has over 800 students from kindergarten to
twelfth grade. Most of the students are Americans. It is coeducational and follows the American curriculum.

- **The International School of Paris**, elementary school: 96 bis rue du Ranelagh, 75016 Paris; tel: 42 24 43 40; high school: 7 rue Chardin, 75016 Paris; tel: 45 27 50 01. Founded in 1964, the International School is coeducational and follows the American curriculum supplemented by a French language and humanities programme. Classes are small, and individual attention is given to each student from four to fourteen (kindergarten to the eighth grade).

- **Marymount International**, 72 boulevard de la Saussaye, 92200 Neuilly; tel: 46 24 10 51 or 47 22 04 35. This coeducational school was founded in 1923. It is Catholic-run, but the teaching is non-sectarian. The school accommodates children from four to thirteen, up to eighth grade. The instruction is given in English with special emphasis on French language and culture. Multi-age grouping is used instead of traditional grades. The enrolment is 350.

## Bilingual schools

- **Montessori School of Paris**, 23 avenue George V, 75008 Paris. The Montessori School of Paris takes children from two-and-a-half to five, September to June, from 9h to 12h. This bilingual school creates a very relaxed learning environment.

- **Ecole Active Bilingue (Ecole Internationale de Paris)** 70, rue de Théatre or 115 avenue Emile Zola, 75015 Paris. This coeducational school is rapidly expanding and now has seven annexes with an enrolment of about 2,500 students. The number for information is 46 22 14 24. The school takes children from kindergarten upwards. French language classes are given to help foreign students adjust until they can follow the French teaching; basic languages are French and English.

- **Lycée International de St Germain en Laye**, rue du Fer à Cheval, 78100 St Germain en Laye; tel: 34 51 94 11. This international school also provides the opportunity for expatriate children to study in a normal French school while taking several courses (literature, language and their own country's history) in their own language. Children start with three to six months of intensive training in special French classes. Then they join other children of their age group, being taught in French by French teachers for part of each day and in English by English-speaking teachers the rest of the time.

**French schools**

If you decide to put your children in a French school, it might be a very exciting experience for them. Obviously, the younger the children, the easier it is for them to adapt to a different system and language. A child under the age of eleven can easily attend a French elementary school. After the first three months he or she will be speaking French fluently. To obtain a list of French public schools in your area, go to the city hall (**mairie**) near your residence.

There are a great many private French schools, some of them day schools, some boarding schools. Contact the French Cultural Services before leaving home for a list. Other useful sources of information are

- **Centre National de l'Enseignement Privé**, 12 boulevard de Courcelles, 75017 Paris; tel: 43 80 89 16 (gives free counselling by appointment).

- **Service d'Information des Familles**, 277 rue St Jacques, 75005 Paris; tel: 43 29 12 77 (guidance, directories).

- **Centre National de Documentation sur l'Enseignement Privé**, 20 rue Fabert, 75007 Paris; tel: 47 05 32 68 (exhaustive lists of all private schools, weekend or holiday boarding facilities; counselling of parents offered: no appointment necessary).

## SPECIAL ADVANTAGES FOR STUDENTS

Full-time students enrolled in a secondary or postsecondary institution (inside or outside France) are granted many special benefits in France (as they are in most European countries): reduced fares on trains and buses; use of cheaper student restaurants; reduced admission to museums, theatres, cultural events and historical sites. Students are a very favoured group and they should take advantage of this fact. To qualify for these benefits students need

- an international student ID card. For this, contact the Council of International Educational Exchange. CIEE has four travel offices in Paris: 49 rue Pierre Charron, 75008 Paris: tel: 43 59 23 69; Centro Franco-Américain Odéon, 1 place de l'Odéon, 75006 Paris; tel: 46 34 16 10; 51 rue Dauphine, 75006 Paris; tel: 43 26 79 65; and 16 rue Vaugirard, 75006 Paris; tel: 46 34 02 90.

- a French student identity card from CROUS (Centre Regional des Ouevres Universitaires et Scolaires), 8 rue Jean Calvin,

75005 Paris. This organisation also has an office in each university town in France.

Students will also find this address very useful: Organisation de Tourisme Universitaire, 137 boulevard St Michel, 75005 Paris; tel: 43 29 12 88.

## OPPORTUNITIES IN HIGHER EDUCATION

Every year some 100,000 foreigners enrol as students in French universities. For entrance the Baccalauréat or a qualification officially recognised as its equivalent is required. For those interested in knowing more about universities in France, contact any of the following:

- **Service National d'Accueil aux Etudiants Etrangers** (Welcome Centre for Foreign Students), 69 Quai d'Orsay, 75007 Paris: information on all aspects of student living, regulations, working conditions, etc.

- **Centre National des Oeuvres Universitaires et Scolaires** (National Centre for University and School Activities) or CNOUS, located at the same address: 8 rue Jean Calvin, 75005 Paris.

- **Office National des Universités et Ecoles Françaises**, 96 boulevard Raspail, 75272 Paris Cedex 06; 42 22 26 95.

- French Embassy Cultural Section, 22 Wilton Crescent, London SW1X 8SB. Tel: (071) 235 8080.

France has more than 200 higher education institutions, including 72 traditional universities. They include the various **écoles** or **grandes écoles** which are not linked to the Ministry of Education and which select students by means of very tough competitive examinations. In addition France has very well-developed facilities for promoting French language and culture, and courses of this nature abound. The academic year runs from October to June.

### 1st degree courses
*Length* Two years for Diploma (DEUG), three for **licence**, four for **maîtrise**.

*Contact*
Ministère de l'Education Nationale, Direction de L'Enseignement Supérieur, Bureau d'information et d'orientation, 61/65 rue Dutot, 75015 Paris. Tel: (010 331) 539 2575 ext 32-79 and 37-47. This is the Ministry of Education information bureau in charge of higher education.

L'Office Nationale d'Information sur les Enseignements et les Professions (ONISEP), 168 boulevard de Montparnasse, 75014 Paris. Has a range of publications for sale and consultation on careers and university studies.

*Applications*
You should apply for university places in December and January each year (final deadline 1st February), on forms available from the French Embassy Cultural Section.

*Entrance requirements*
Minimum two 'A' levels and three GCSEs, or other equivalent of French Baccalauréat. There are no entrance exams. Knowledge of French is required; this can be brought to an acceptable level by attending a course specially laid on for this purpose before the beginning of the academic year (see Language Courses below). Tests can be taken either in the UK (apply to French Embassy Cultural Section, as above) or at the first university of your choice.

*Costs/grants*
Tuition costs are minimal: a total of approximately £80 should cover all tuition and registration fees.


**Postgraduate**
Postgraduate students coming from the British system would take either the one year **maîtrise** (see above) or a doctorate (three years), or a one year professional qualification (DESS).

*Contact*
The universities themselves. Lists may be obtained from Ministry of Education or Embassy; see above.

*Entrance requirements*
Minimum requirement is a good Bachelor's degree.

*Grants*
For French Government scholarships in the Arts (French language and culture, and performance arts) contact Service Culturel, 22

Wilton Crescent, as above. For French Government scholarships in scientific fields (applied biotechnology, materials science and composites and microelectronics only), contact Scientific Counsellor, French Embassy, Silver City House, 62 Brompton Road, London SW3 1BW. In both cases applications must be made by mid January, through your university department if you are currently studying in the UK.

Research fellowships and short-term research bursaries in science or humanities are offered to Britsh postgraduates *with some research experience* by the **Centre National de la Recherche Scientifique**. Apply to British Council, OEAD, 65 Davies Street, London W1Y 2AA, by March.

Scholarships for French studies are offered by the British Institute in Paris. Apply to the Secretary, British Institute in Paris, Senate House, Malet Street, London WC1H 7HU.

Exchange fellowships in the field of biomedical research; apply to the Training Awards Group, Medical Research Council, 20 Park Crescent, London W1N 4AL.

The **Centre Nationale des Oeuvres Universitaires et Scolaires** (CNOUS), 69 Quai d'Orsay, 75007 Paris, has special responsibility for foreign students and grants available to them in France.

### Visiting studentships in France
Contact CROUS **(Centres Régionaux des Oeuvres Universitaires et Scolaires)**, 39 ave Georges Bernanos, Paris 75005.


## LANGUAGE COURSES

The Service Culturel (see above) can send you a booklet entitled *Cours de Français pour étudiants étrangers.* It is published annually and lists French language courses up and down the country open to foreign students, including those run by or in conjunction with universities, and those offered by private organisations. The information given includes the type of course, its organisation, dates, costs and practical information on student life, as well as contact addresses. Courses range from language courses for complete beginners to university level courses leading to recognised diplomas; the wide choice means that you should be able to find a course to suit your exact requirements in terms of level, timing, and so forth. Specialist courses are run for students intending to start regular university courses in France, non-native teachers of French, and people needing French for special purposes.

This information comes in French. Similar information in English is contained in *Study Holidays* published by the Central Bureau for Educational Visits and Exchanges in London. A few examples are as follows:

Courses run by the **Alliance Française**—an important French teaching association with branches worldwide. See below for the address of the London branch. In France write to one of the following addresses:

1 rue Vernier, 0600 Nice. Tel: 87 42 11.
101 boulevard Raspail, 75270 Paris. Tel: 45 44 38 28.
32 rue de Buffon, 76000 Rouen. Tel: 08 55 99.
9 place du Capitole, 31000 Toulouse. Tel: 23 41 24.

Courses are run by well known private language teaching organisations, such as **Eurocentres**, 13 passage Dauphine, 75006 Paris, tel: 43 25 81 40; 10 rue Amelot, 17000 La Rochelle, tel: 50 57 33; 1 avenue Léonard de Vinci, 37400 Amboise; tel: 23 10 60. **Inlingua**, 109 rue l'Université, 75007 Paris, tel: 51 46 60; 8 rue de Coëtguen, Place de la Mairie, 35000 Rennes, tel: 51 46 60. There are many other private language schools much too numerous to list.

### UK offices for French language courses

Some schools have offices or agents in the UK through which you can book courses:

Institut Britannique de Paris, London Office, University of London, Senate House, Room 215, Malet Street, London WC1E 7HU. Tel: (071) 636 8000 ext 3920.

Inlingua School of Languages, 8-10 Rotton Park Road, Edgbaston, Birmingham B16 9JJ. Tel: (021) 454 0204.

Eurolanguage, Greyhound House, 23-24 George Street, Richmond, Surrey, TW9 1HY. Tel: (081) 940 1087.

Youth Travels Abroad, 117 Wendell Road, London W12 9SD. Tel: (081) 743 7966.

En Famille Agency (Overseas), Westbury House, Queens Lane, Arundel, West Sussex BN18 9JN. Tel: Arundel 883266.

School Travel Service, 24 Colloden Road, Enfield, Middlesex EN2 8QD. Tel (081) 363 8202.

Scholatravel, 8 South Parade, Weston-super-Mare, BS23 1JN. Tel: (0934) 29037.

French Government Tourist Office, Youth Travel Dept (see below).

## Summer schools

Programmes of study in French language, literature, theatre, music, art and so forth are run by:

Académie International d'Eté, 89 bis avenue Sainte-Marie, 94016 Sainte-Mande.

Cours Universitaire d'Eté Saint Malo, Université Haute Bretagne, 6 avenue Gaston Berger, 35043 Rennes. Tel: 54 99 55.

## Joint programmes/special schemes

ERASMUS.

## Welfare

Special travel concessions and student social security covering medical expenses.

## Other useful addresses

- French Government Tourist Office, 178 Piccadilly, London W1V 0AL. Tel: (071) 491 7622.
- Alliance Française, 6 Cromwell Place, London SW7 2JN. Tel: (071) 723 6439.
- Institut Français, 14 Cromwell Place, London SW7 2JR. Tel: (071) 581 2701. Also in Edinburgh.
- Ministère de l'Education Nationale, 110 rue de Grenelle, 75357 Paris. Tel: 45 50 10 10.

*Student travel*
OTU, 137 boulevard St Michel, 75005 Paris.

# 9
# Getting Around

## CARS

France has an enormous road network which the French say could 'girdle the world seventeen times'. There are more than 930,000 miles of roads, including modern motorways (**autoroutes**); the former main roads (**routes nationales**), which are usually lined with poplars or plane trees; and the picturesque secondary roads (**routes départementales**), where tourists rarely venture and which are perfect for cyclists. Tolls are payable on French motorways.

Although you will often use the excellent trains for long distances and leave your car in the garage during the week (if you live in a large city), you will probably be very happy to have a car at other times. Nothing can beat a car for exploring out-of-the-way places in France or the rest of Europe.

### Entry of vehicles into France
You can either bring your car into the country or buy one after you arrive. If you go to France as a visitor with your car and stay less than six months, you do not need a customs document for it. You will, however, need

- an international driving licence (but see page 32)
- car insurance valid in France

If you buy the car in France and pay in foreign currency, you can use (for a maximum of six months) a temporary TT licence plate.

If you plan to become a temporary resident of France, you can bring your previously owned car(s) in tax free within one year of your arrival in France. Incidentally, you can also bring in, duty free, a number of other vehicles: camper, motorcycle, camping trailer, private tourist plane, or pleasure boat. These imports are allowed if the vehicles have been **the personal property of the importer for at least six months and will not be sold for six months after their entry into France.** You should inform the French consulate in your area before your departure that you intend to import property and ask about required documentation.

Most people prefer to have a small European-made car: it is easier to get parts and make repairs, the savings on fuel will be appreciable since French petrol is expensive, and driving and parking in narrow medieval streets is impossible with a big car.

## Registration

As a resident in France, you need French licence plates (**plaques d'immatriculation**), for which you apply to the **préfecture de police**. They will send you a registration number, which you take to a private garage, which in turn makes up the plates and installs them for a fee. The most practical way to document your vehicle and obtain the registration papers (**carte grise**) is to apply to the Automobile Club d'Ile de France, 8 place de la Concorde, 75008 Paris; tel: 42 66 43 00, or to any of its representatives in most cities of France.

For more precise information on registration, licensing, car insurance and other problems, contact any of the following organisations:

- AAA, 8 rue de la Paix, 75002 Paris;

- Automobile Club d'Ile de France, 8 place de la Concorde, 75008 Paris: tel: 42 66 43 00;

- Touring Club de France, 14 avenue de la Grande Armée, 75017 Paris: tel: 43 80 68 58.

## Licence

To obtain a French driving licence, go to the closest **préfecture** (if living in the provinces) or to the **préfecture de police** (if living in Paris), 7 boulevard du Palais, 75004 Paris, Métro: Cité. EC licence holders do not need to pass a French driving test providing they exchange their licence within 12 months of arrival.

## Insurance

If you are bringing a car into the country, you must get an insurance certificate from your insurer before leaving home. Ask the French consulate. All visitors to France except EC citizens must produce either an international insurance certificate ('green card'), an

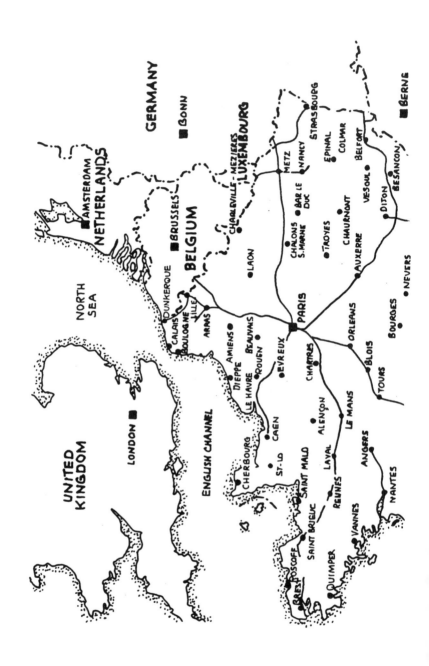

GERMANY

BONN

NETHERLANDS
AMSTERDAM

BRUSSELS

BELGIUM

LUXEMBOURG

CHARLEVILLE-MEZIERES

STRASBOURG

METZ
NANCY

EPINAL
COLMAR

BELFORT

VESOUL

DITON

BESANCON

BERNE

BAR LE DUC

CHALONS
S. MARNE

TROYES

CHAUMONT

AUXERRE

NEVERS

LAON

NORTH
SEA

DUNKERQUE

LILLE

ARRAS

CALAIS

BOULOGNE

PARIS

ORLEANS

BOURGES

AMIENS

BEAUVAIS

ROUEN

EVREUX

CHARTRES

BLOIS

TOURS

DIEPPE

LE HAVRE

LONDON

CAEN

ALENCON

LE MANS

ANGERS

NANTES

CHERBOURG

ST-LO

SAINT MALO

LAVAL

RENNES

VANNES

UNITED
KINGDOM

ENGLISH CHANNEL

SAINT BRIEUC

ROSCOFF

QUIMPER

BREST

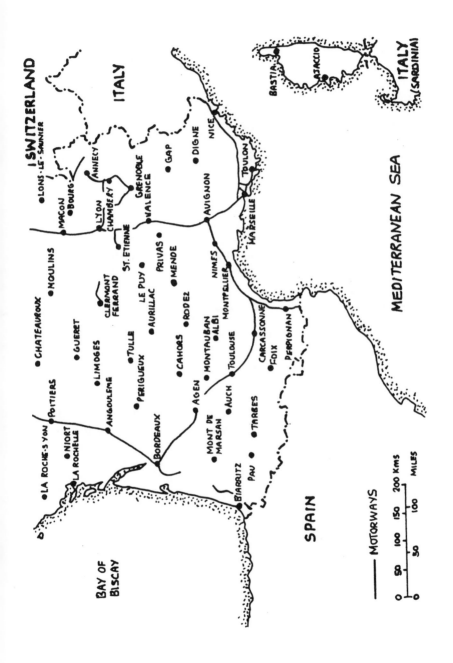

insurance certificate issued by a French company on arrival at the point of entry, or a short-term policy issued at the border (**assurance-frontière**).

Third-party motor insurance for unlimited liability is compulsory in France, and premiums are very expensive. Insurance policies are not standardized and conditions and costs vary enormously from company to company. It is wise to shop around for the best terms. Some companies grant a non-claims bonus.

Your best bet is to deal through an insurance broker, who gives you individualised service (and the price to go with it). For guidance contact the Centre de Documentation et d'Information sur les Assurances, 2 rue Chaussée d'Antin, 75009 Paris; tel: 48 24 96 12.

### Some unfamiliar rules of the road

Driving rules are complicated. Get the motor department book of rules (*Code de la Route*), available in English, and study it well. Points regarding right-of-way, behaviour at intersections and parking which you would take for granted at home may be different in France, and the police are quite aggressive in their enforcement.

Flash your headlights as you approach an intersection. **Never** sound your horn in a town, it is absolutely forbidden. If you are passing on the open road, however, you must warn by either horn or lights as well as by using directional signals. Use only parking lights at night when driving in town or on lighted highways. Speed limits are strict and should be carefully observed. One drives on the right and passes on the left. Wearing seatbelts is required by law on French motorways, and children under ten are not permitted to ride in the front seat at any time (even a baby on a lap). Both these offences are punishable by a fine. Yellow headlight bulbs and directional signals are compulsory on vehicles registered in France. Furthermore, France has strict rules that limit vehicle interference with radio and TV reception. You may have to install radio/TV interference suppressing equipment on imported cars.

- **Parking**. Parking is, on the whole, tight and difficult. **Zone Bleue** (Blue Zone) parking is restricted to 90 minutes (9h to 19h) except on holidays. You buy a parking disc and put it in your car window with the time marked on it. Discs are bought at various newsstands and small shops—ask locally.

- **Tickets**. Paris makes it easy for you to pay parking fines—most tickets are payable by mail, using stamps which you buy for the purpose from the nearest tobacconist shop.

- **Accidents**. Whenever you drive, always carry your valid insurance certificate; it is vitally important. Report any accident at once to your insurance company, giving the name, address, licence and insurance company of the other party involved—witnesses too if possible. Also call the Automobile Club if you are a member. In towns get a police officer to make a report (**dresser un constat**). In the country, if there has been personal injury, advise the police. If you are the holder of a 'green card', immediately inform the Bureau Central Français d'Assurances contre les Accidents d'Automobiles (Central French Insurance Office against Car Accidents), 118 rue de Tocqueville, 75017 Paris.

### Petrol
Petrol is sold by the litre. 2-star and 4-star are **ordinaire** and **super-carburant**, respectively. To ask for a fill-up, you say, 'Le plein, s'il vous plaît.'

## TRAINS

### TGV
Trains in France are excellent and numerous and they run on time. The state-owned company is called SNCF (**Société Nationale des Chemins de Fer Français**, meaning National Society of French Railways). The SNCF is proud of its newest train, the TGV (**Train Grande Vitesse**, 'very high speed') which, at 265 miles per hour, is the fastest train in the world.

At first the TGV ran only a short stretch from Paris to Lyon. It now links the capital with the Mediterranean, Switzerland, and the west and north of France. Soon, Brussels will be only one-and-a-half hours from Paris and London not much further way when the TGV crosses the Channel Tunnel to England.

### Reservations
It is wise to make reservations ahead of time rather than waiting until just before departure when stations may be crowded. Make reservations by phoning the stations or by calling the Bureau de Tourisme de la SNCF, 16 boulevard des Capucines, 75009 Paris; tel: 47 42 00 26. The bureau also has useful brochures, such as the *Guide Pratique du Voyageur* (Practical Guide for the Traveller). A ticket is good for two months. Reservations are compulsory on many French trains, including all TGVs.

## Night trains

If you travel by night, you can use **couchettes** with six bunks in second class or with four bunks in first class. Some trains have **voiture-lits** (sleepers) with one, two or three beds. Not all trains have a **wagon-restaurant** (dining car), so check ahead of time.

No one checks tickets as you board a train, but you have to punch (**composter**) your ticket yourself before you reach the platform. If you want to leave your baggage in the station, look for the **consigne** (left luggage).

## Special fares

It is well worth inquiring at one of the SNCF offices or the French National Railways headquarters in London about the many special fares and services they offer.

- **For nonresidents** France-Vacances, Eurailpass, and Eurail Youth Pass give unlimied travel for their periods of validity.

- **For residents**
  –children under four travel free;
  –children four to twelve travel half-price;
  –with a **carte-jeune** (card for young people) one travels at half-price;
  –with a card **inter-rail** bought in France those under twenty-six can travel anywhere in France for one month at half-price; bought outside France it offers a month of unlimited travel in France (and elsewhere in Europe).
  –a card **couple-famille** (couple-family) qualifies the holder to a 50 per cent rebate when two members of the family travel together;
  –with a card **vermeille** (over sixty) seniors can travel at half- price.

## BUSES, BOATS AND BARGES

Touring France by bus can be very pleasant. Incidentally, an **autobus** is a city bus, but a coach driving in the country is called a **car** or an **autocar**. You can plan a trip either by using the regularly scheduled buses or by joining a tour group through a travel agent or tour operator.

In recent years boat and barge travel have become extremely popular. You can reserve a most comfortable room on a luxuriously decorated barge. Grande cuisine is served, and fresh croissants are brought to you for breakfast. Or you can choose a cheaper boat you drive yourself to discover the canals of France.

Several travel companies organise tours on the French canals—contact tourist offices. A useful book about canal tours, *Le Tourisme Fluvial en France*, is available from Ministère de l'Equipement, Direction des Ports Maritimes et Voies Navigables, Service d'Information et des Relations Publiques, 244 boulevard St Germain, 75007 Paris.

# 10
# Leisure Time

Leisure time is given great importance in France, perhaps more so than in many other countries. France is probably the only country to have a Ministry of free time, **Ministère de Temps Libre, de la Jeunesse et des Sports**. Information on many leisure activities will inevitably tend to centre around Paris. Paris is the focus for all sorts of activities in France, as London is the focus in the UK. However, the attractions of other regions will also be investigated.

## Sports

Sports facilities, which used to be limited to major cities and resorts, exist now in smaller towns and even in the country. Traditional sports are still very much in favour; biking, walking (called **footing** in French), playing **boules** (bowls), fishing and hunting.

Soccer is the most popular French game, both to watch and to play. Tennis is reaching all sectors of the population; public courts are being built, and private clubs are multiplying.

Boxing and basketball are popular. Golf is still an exclusive sport but good courses can be found around large cities and tourist areas. There is skiing in the Alps and the Pyrenees. Fresh water and deep-sea fishing are available. The Paris area, with several race courses, is a dream for horse racing enthusiasts. Jogging is popular with people of all ages. Riding is available almost anywhere.

If you enjoy water sports, you'll love France. Swimming is a very popular sport along the coast or in rivers and pools. Sailing has become the passion of many French. Yacht harbours and sailing marinas are springing up everywhere. Waterskiing is popular, of course, but windsurfing is the sport of the day. You will see hundreds of windsurfers, of all ages, on the beaches; they are getting more and more daring and now use shorter boards to jump over the waves and the surf.

Information on all sports is readily available and can be obtained from tourist offices, from the national federation of each particular sport, or from the Ministry of Youth and Sports. Call **Direction du Temps Libre et de l'Education Populaire** (Direction des Sports), 78 rue Olivier de Serres, 75739 Paris Cedex 15; tel: 48 28 40 40. The Club Mediterranée, with vacation villages in France and other countries, offers sailing, riding, skiing, scuba-diving, etc. The address in France is Place de la Bourse, 75002 Paris; tel: 42 96 10 00.

## THE ARTS AND ENTERTAINMENT

### Museums
As you are probably aware, France is wonderful for museum lovers. Museums are numerous and the exhibits usually of high quality. With few exceptions, museums are open all day, everyday except Tuesdays. National museums are half-price on Wednesdays and Sundays (avoid the latter in summer). Most charge an entrance fee. A good time to go is lunchtime when the French are eating.

- **The Louvre**, on the banks of the Seine, is in the world's largest royal palace. To see every room of this massive museum, which has recently been renovated and much enlarged, takes a week or more. Every day at 10h 30 and 15h there are guided tours in French and English.

- **Galerie du Jeu de Paume** is a small, delightful museum at the place de la Concorde, with a collection of impressionist and early cubist paintings.

- **Musée National d'Art Moderne** has contemporary painting and sculpture: Picasso, Braque, Roualt, Dufy, Calder, Kandinsky, etc.

- **Centre National d'Art et de Culture Georges Pompidou** permanently displays about 2,000 works of twentieth-century artists and twice a year organises a major special exhibit.

- **Musée Rodin** is located in an elegant eighteenth-century residence surrounded by vast gardens restored to their original form. It contains works by the famous nineteenth-century French sculptor, Rodin.

- **Musée d'Orsay**, a huge, old glass and steel railway station, contains nineteenth-century works of art.

- **Musée Picasso** is located in a lovely private residence—the Hôtel Sale—of the Marais district.

- The **Cité des Sciences et de l'Industrie**, at La Villette, has just recently opened and is a spectacular and futuristic museum of science and industry, probably the largest in the world.

**Son et Lumière** offers sound and light spectacles of which the French were the originators. They are presented at many historic sites in Paris and the provinces: les Invalides in Paris, *châteaux* in the Loire valley, the Palais des Papes in Avignon, etc.

NB **La Carte** is a pass giving 50% discount on admission to about 60 national and municipal museums in the Paris area. The card can be purchased at the museums it covers and is valid for 1, 3, or 5 days at varying prices. For details, contact the French Government Tourist Office (see end of chapter).

### Theatre
In the city of Paris and its inner suburbs there are about 150 theatre workshops, some of which often have several shows running simultaneously. The **Comédie Française**, one of the most famous, has a classical repertory and is one of six state-subsidised theatres. It is wise to reserve your seat in advance of a performance. Tickets will cost between 30 and 150FF in a national or subsidised theatre and between 50 and 100FF in a private theatre. Midweek *matinée* subscriptions may be obtained at a reduced rate while the City of Paris has the **Théâtre Kiosk** found on Place de Madeleine which sells cheap places for the day's shows. Students can also get cut-price seats from the Cultural Service of CROUS (see 'Education in France').

The French Punch and Judy theatre is based in Lyon which also has at least 50 modern theatre companies. The *Lyon Libération* has details of local programmes and is thought to be the most culturally orientated newspaper in the area.

There are, of course, theatres to be found in all regions of France. Contact your local Tourist Information Office for details.

### Music
Paris has many concert halls. Salle Pleyel, Salle Gaveau, Salle du Conservatoire de Musique, and Théâtre des Champs Elysées are among the best known. The Opéra has full-length operas. A second Opéra near the bastille has just been completed. Operas such as *Carmen* or *Madame Butterfly* and light operas are often performed

at the Salle Favart (formerly the Opéra Comique); musical comedies are performed at the Théâtre Mogador and the Théâtre Musical de Paris.

Special prices at concerts for young people (under 30) are available through JMF (**Jeunesses Musicales de France**) 14 rue François Miron, 75004 Paris, and Les Activités Musicales de Jeunes, 252 Faubourg St Honoré, 75016 France.

## Cinema

There are about five hundred cinemas located in and around Paris. With few exceptions, the huge theatres of the past have been replaced by a clutter of small theatres. Foreign films are shown in their original languages (**version originale**) on the Champs Elysées and in the Left Bank area. Besides being enjoyable, watching French movies is an excellent way to improve one's language ability—many people have learned a lot of French by paying close attention to films and TV.

## Programmes

At all newspaper stands you will find *Une Semaine à Paris* and *Pariscope* (every Wednesday) or *Paris Weekly Information* (in English), also *L'Officiel des Spectacles*. For music programmes, check the *Guide des Concerts* or *Les Activités Musicales*. For round-the-clock information (in English) on leisure activities, phone 47 20 88 98.

## NOT TO MISS IN PARIS

- **Open air markets**. You will enjoy the lively and tempting food markets which operate every day in many streets: boulevard Raspail, avenue de Versailles, rue de Buci and many others. There are also specialized markets for any taste or interest: bird and flower markets and several huge flea markets. Stamp collectors meet twice a week near the Rond-Point des Champs Elysées.

- **Friday nights at the Louvre**. Many of the great sculpture galleries are specially illuminated on Friday evenings.

- **Dancing in the streets**. On the nights of July 13, 14, and 15, each area of Paris has its own open-air ball. July 14 (Bastille Day) offers fireworks in five different parts of the city at 22h.

- **Trip down the Seine**. The Bâteaux Mouche offer daily trips every half hour. They have restaurants on board. They dock at Alma Bridge on the Right Bank of the river (phone 42 25 96 10).

- **Walks through Paris**. One can walk forever in Paris. Discover the new Paris: visit the Palais des Congrès, near avenue de la Grande Armée; climb the Tour Montparnasse, the highest new building in Paris, on the Left Bank; or wander through the many levels of the Forum des Halles. You can also study the history of Paris through its historic buidings, former private mansions, its old quarters (**quartiers**), and the nearby **châteaux**. Get in touch with the Monuments Historiques, 62 rue St Antoine, 75004 Paris; tel: 42 74 22 22.

## HOBBIES, CLUBS AND OTHER ACTIVITIES

Almost any hobby can be pursued in France; photography, ceramics, weaving, painting or collecting antiques, to mention but a few. A wide choice of musical instruments or stereo and video equipment is available, although they are probably more expensive than in Germany or Britain.

The Jockey Club is 'High Society'—aristocratic, expensive and hard to get in. Other popular clubs include the International Club, the Racing Club of France, Rotary clubs, and Lions clubs. Most businesspeople who golf belong to golf clubs in the Paris area. A social club for many businesspeople to join is the Club des Cent. Inquire locally for clubs in other cities.

### Other activities

- **The language and the civilisation**. You *must* learn French in order to have real friends among the French or, indeed, much fun in the French world. An excellent way to spend your first months is to take courses in the language, history, arts, and architecture of France (according to your interests) at the Louvre, Sorbonne or elsewhere several mornings a week. The benefits are twofold: (1) you can acclimatise yourself to France and French culture in the quickest possible way, and (2) you will have a chance to meet others with similar interests, including many French as well as other foreigners like yourself. Paris has many art and music schools. The most famous is Ecole du Louvre, place Carrousel, 75001 Paris, which offers art appreciation courses on a non-degree basis. Also worth mentioning (for the specialists) are the Ecole Nationale Supérieure des Arts Décoratifs, tel: 43 29 86 79 and the Conservatoire National Supérieur de Musique, tel: 42 93 15 20; both are on the Left Bank.

- **Making friends.** Don't expect to be invited into French homes readily—especially until you speak French. Your first and easiest friendships can be found among other internationals—Canadians, Americans, Australians, Italians, Germans, etc as well as British, most of whom will also be looking for friends. If you are sports-minded, join the sports clubs of your interest. This is one of the best ways to meet lively people with interests similar to yours. Whether or not you are by nature a joiner, it is a good idea to seek out congenial groups when you go to a new country—musicians, photographers, bird-watchers, stamp collectors, or whatever.

- **Volunteering.** Volunteering is not a familiar concept in France. However, you can do volunteer work through various international groups or an association of 'friends of museums'. Explore along your lines of interest, asking everyone you meet what they suggest, or develop some projects of your own.

## ACTIVITIES FOR CHILDREN

Again, it is best to inquire at your local Tourist Office for zoos, parks etc located near your home. There are many things for young children to do in Paris: most parks (Tuileries, Luxembourg, Champs Elysées, Monceau, etc) have puppet shows, donkey rides, playgrounds, and roundabouts. Children can hire little sailing boats and use them on ponds. The Jardin d'Acclimatation in the Bois de Boulogne is a great attraction for children; it has a zoo, a large amusement park and a long miniature train. There is an African game preserve at the Château de Thoiry, forty kilometres west of Paris, where animals run free behind moats. It is open from 11h to dark.

Some of the museums most popular with children are:

- **Musée de la Marine-Aquarium**, Palais de Chaillot, 75016 Paris;
- **Palais de la Découverte**, avenue Franklin Roosevelt, 75008 Paris;
- **Planetarium** (experiments in physics, chemistry, etc), in Palais de la Découverte, 75008 Paris;

- **Musée Grévin** (wax museum), 10 boulevard Montmarte, 75009 Paris;
- **Musée des Arts et Traditions Populaires** (folk arts and traditions), near Palaise de Chaillot and Eiffel Tower, 75016 Paris.

There are several children's theatres. The best known is the Théâtre du Petit Monde, 252 Faubourg St Honoré, 75002 Paris, open every Wednesday and Sunday. There are also films and concerts for chidren.

Many family resorts have **clubs de plage** to care for children, ages four to twelve. There are special clubs and classes at many ski resorts and special living arrangements for children of families on vacation. The Club Meditérranée has 'villages' where activities are organised especially for small children.

## EATING OUT

It can be difficult to find places to eat which are both of good quality and relatively inexpensive, especially when you are a newcomer. In time, you will probably hear by word of mouth which **restaurants** are the most popular in your area. Recommendations from locals are often the most reliable.

Generally, restaurants offer a choice between meals at a fixed price chosen from a menu or **à la carte** selection. If you choose the **prix fixe**, you will be able to eat more economically. Service should be included and a beverage such as ¼ litre wine or some mineral water will often be provided as part of such a meal. An inexpensive meal will include an appetiser, main course, cheese or dessert. If something to drink is not included, you do not have to buy anything if you do not want to; it is perfectly acceptable to ask for **une carafe d'eau**, a jug of water.

If you choose to eat à la carte, however, you can make your selection from the various choices appearing on the menu. This is the more expensive option and drinks and service (around 15%) will be added to the price of the food.

*NB* Always check whether service is included (**servis compris**) in fixed price or à la carte meals. **Servis non compris** means that service is *not* included.

In a **café**, you can get a drink at the counter (**au comptoir**) or at a table (**en salle**), the latter being more expensive as the price will include service. You will also be able to get both hot and cold food such as sandwiches, toasted food or an omelette. Some cafés may have more substantial meals available such as steak and chips. It is relatively inexpensive to eat in a café or what the French call a snack bar. Cafés with a red **tabac** sign also sell all sorts of items from postage stamps to tax stamps (**vignettes**).

**Fast food** is becoming increasingly popular in France. Many American companies such as MacDonald's have outlets as well as several French franchises: Rouge Blanc, Espace Gourmand and many more.

Here are some recommended places to eat:

### Bordeaux

- *L'Aiguille de Pin*, 253 rue Judaïque.
- *Café du Musée*, rue Foy.
- *L'Ombrière*, 14 Place du Parlement.

### Lille

- *Balatum*, 13 rue Barré.
- *Bolée*, 12 rue Thiers.

### Lyon

- *Bistroquet*, 42 rue Sala.
- *La Rose des Vins*, 5 rue de la Fromagerie.
- *Cycéron*, 54 rue Mercière.

### Strasbourg

- *Brasserie de la Victoire*, Quai des Pêcheurs.
- *Au Petit Bois Vert*, 3 Quai de la Bruche.

### Marseille

- *Chez Alex*, 43 rue Curiol.
- *Al Grisino*, 21 cours Julien.

### Rennes

- *L'Opus*, 24 rue de la Chalotais.
- *Le Panier a Salades*, 15 rue de Penhoët.

If you are dining at someone's house, it is generally considered polite to acknowledge the invitation by writing and flowers are appropriate to take as a present.

Generally speaking, whether you are having a meal at someone else's home, or entertaining guests yourself, the 'rules' are much like those governing dinner party etiquette in the UK. If this is something you are particularly concerned about, buy yourself a guide to the subject once resident in France.

If you prefer to do your eating and drinking in less formal ways, France is not short on nightlife. Call in on local tourist offices for information on pubs and clubs. Local event magazines and newspapers also give details on what's available in the area.

## HOLIDAYING IN FRANCE

France is one of the most popular tourist countries of the world. Any travel agent can present you with a multitude of tours. But, as a resident of France, you have the advantage of already being there; you can plan your own trip and avoid the millions of cars which crowd French roads in July and August every year.

Many excellent guidebooks are available. The best known French guidebooks are

- *Green Michelin Guide* (English edition)—makes a very detailed study of cities or regions, giving the history, architecture and the arts.
- *Red Michelin Guide of France*—identifies hotels and restaurants (graded by quality and price) and provides a map of each town for motorists.
- *Blue Guide*—gives detailed itineraries; culturally oriented for the scholar and art lover (published in France, but also available in the UK).

If you plan a trip out of the high season (July and August), you can gamble on finding accommodation without reservations, especially if you get off the beaten track and drive on secondary roads. Otherwise, do make reservations ahead of time.

Accommodation can vary from a luxurious suite in a historic castle or a modest room in a farmhouse or a reasonably priced but comfortable family-type hotel. The following organisations can be most helpful to you in planning your holiday throughout France:

- **Fédération Nationale des Logis et Auberges de France** (dwellings and inns of France), 25 rue Jean Mermoz, 75008 Paris; tel: 43

59 86 67), offers accommodation in small hotels and modest rural inns.

- **Fédération Nationale des Gîtes Ruraux de France** (*gîte* means a humble dwelling), 34 rue Godot de Mauroy, 75009 Paris; tel: 47 42 25 43, offers the equivalent of bed and breakfast. This organisation enables you to see France from a really grassroots level; farm families offer accommodation in their homes, and they must meet approved standards.

- **France-accueil** (France welcome), 46 boulevard Côte Blatin, 63010 Clermond Ferrand, Cedex; tel: 73 93 92 50, lists one- or two-star hotel chains throughout France.

- **Châteaux et Hôtels de France**, 11 rue de Boétie, Paris 75008, and **Relais et Châteaux**, Hôtel Crillon, 10 place de la Concorde, Paris 75008, offer large, comfortable and expensive (but fascinating) places to stay.

In general, you can spend your holiday in France in almost any kind of way. From lying on a hot beach to a strenuous activity type holiday; from festivals to boating holidays; from a variety of 'special interest' holidays to traditional family ones, it's all available. Your local tourist office will be able to give you details of the holidays mentioned here as well as many more. For information on home leisure activities, for those preferring to spend their holidays in their new French residences, again contact the tourist office, local leisure centres, newspaper and event magazines. Your town hall (**mairie**) can also be a useful source of information and may be able to help if you are interested in joining local clubs, societies or centres. Whatever your hobby or interest, you should be able to pursue it as a resident of France.

**L'Office de Tourisme de Paris** will give you a lot of useful information regarding leisure time activities and events and should also be able to furnish you with the addresses of regional tourist offices giving the same sort of information on provincial areas.

# Useful Contacts

## EMBASSIES AND CONSULATES

The British Embassy, 35 rue du Faubourg St Honoré, 75008 Paris. Tel: 42 66 91 42.

The British Embassy (Consular Section), 109 rue du Faubourg St Honoré, 75008 Paris. Tel: 42 66 91 42.

French Embassy, 58 Knightsbridge, London SW1. Tel: (071) 235 8080.

French Consulate-General, 24 Rutland Gate, London SW7. Tel: (071) 581 5292. Visas and information office: 28-31 Wright's Lane, London W8. Tel: (071) 937 1202.

## TRAVEL

### Contacts in Britain

Air France, 158 New Bond Street, London W1Y 0AY. Tel: (071) 499 9511 (offices also in Birmingham, Manchester and Glasgow).

British Airways Travel Division, PO Box 115, West London Air Terminal, Cromwell Road, London SW7 4ED. Tel: (071) 370 4255.

British Rail Continental Enquiries. Tel: (071) 834 2345.

Brittany Ferries, Millbay Docks, Plymouth PL1 3EF. Tel: (0752) 224921.

Brymon European Airways, 2245 Coventry Road, Birmingham B26 3NG. Tel: (0345) 555800.

French Government Tourist Office, 178 Piccadilly, London W1V 0AL. Tel: (071) 491 7622.

French Railways Ltd, 179 Piccadilly, London W1V 0BA. Tel: (071) 409 3518.

P&O European Ferries, Channel House, Channel View Road, Dover CT17 9TJ. Tel: (0304) 203388.

Sealink British Ferries, PO Box 29, Victoria Station, London SW1V 1JX. Tel: (071) 834 8122.

## Contacts in France

AAA (motoring organisation), 8 rue de la Paix, 75002 Paris.

Automobile Club d'Ile de France, 8 place de la Concorde, 75008 Paris. Tel: 42 66 43 00.

Bicyclub de France, 8 place de la Porte Champerret, 75017 Paris. Tel: 47 66 55 92.

Bureau de Tourisme de la SNCF, 18 boulevard des Capucines, 75009 Paris. Tel: 47 42 00 26. For train reservations, timetables and brochures.

Centre d'Information et de Documentation Jeunesse (CIDJ), 101 quai Branly, 75740 Paris Cedex 15.

Centre Information Jeunesse (CIJ), Parvis de la Préfecture, 1 place des Arts, BP315, 95027 Cergy-Pointoise Cedex.

Centre National des Oeuvres Universitaires et Scolaires (National Centre for University and School Activities), 8 rue Jean Calvin, 75005 Paris.

Châteaux et Hôtels de France, 11 rue de la Boetie, Paris 75008.

France Acceuil (official welcome information offices throughout France). Head office: 85 rue Dessous des Berges, 75013 Paris.

Office de Tourisme de Paris, 127 avenue des Champs Elysées, 75008 Paris. Tel: 47 23 61 72.

Organisation pour la Tourisme Universitaire (OTU), 137 boulevard St Michel, 75005 Paris. Tel: 43 29 12 88. Will issue a FIYTO card to under-26s (Federation of International Youth Travel Organisations).

Service National d'Acceuil aux Etudiants Etrangers (National Welcome Centre for Foreign Students), 69 quai d'Orsay, 75007 Paris.

SNCF Central Information service (French Railways). Tel: 45 82 50 50.

Paris-Velo (bicycle hire), 2 rue Fer-à-Moulin, 75005 Paris. Tel: 43 37 59 22.

Syndicats d'Initiative. The network of French tourist bureaux found in most towns.

Touring Club de France, 14 avenue de la Grande Armée, 75017 Paris. Tel: 43 66 68 58.

## Accommodation (contact organisations)

Acceuil des Jeunes en France, 119 rue St Martin, 75004 Paris. Tel: 42 77 87 80.

Association pour le Logement des Jeunes Travailleurs, 10 rue de Volga, 75020 Paris. Tel: 43 56 27 47.

Comité Nationale des Unions Chrétiennes de Jeunes Gens (YMCA), Résidence Sienne, 5 place de la Venetie, 75643 Paris Cedex 13. Tel: 45 83 62 63.

Contacts-Intervac, 55 rue Nationale, 37000 Tours. Tel: 47 20 20 57. Home exchanges.

Fédération Française de Camping-Caravanning, 78 rue de Rivoli, 75004 Paris. Tel: 42 72 84 08.

Fédération Française des Maisons de Jeunes et de la Culture, 15 rue Condamine, 75017 Paris. Tel: 43 87 30 04.

Fédération Nationale Leo Lagrange, 21 rue de Provence, 75009 Paris. Tel: 42 46 82 92.

Fédération Unie des Auberges de Jeunesse (FUAJ), 6 rue de Mesnil, 75016 Paris. Tel: 45 05 13 14. Will issue an International Youth Hostel Card.

Fondation Nationale de la Cité Universitaire, 19 boulevard Jordan, 75690 Paris. Tel: 45 89 68 52. Campus accommodation for foreign university students.

Home Exchange International, 9 avenue de la Mesange, 94100 St Maur-des-Fosses. Tel: 48 72 92 80.

Ligue Française des Auberges de Jeunesse, 38 boulevard Raspail, 75007 Paris. Tel: 45 48 69 84.

Office du Tourisme Universitaire (OTU), 137 boulevard St Michel, 75005 Paris. Tel: 43 29 11 88.

Séjours, Les Sycomores des Logissons, 13770 Venelles. Tel: 42 61 05 57. Home exchanges.

Union des Centres de Rencontres Internationales de France (UCRIF), 21 rue Beranger, 75003 Paris. Tel: 42 77 08 65.

Union des Fédérations Regionales des Maisons de Jeunes et de la Culture, 168 bis, rue Cardinet, 75017 Paris. Tel: 46 27 79 74.

Union des Foyers de Jeunes Travailleurs (UFJT), 12 avenue Général de Gaulle, 94300 Vincennes. Tel: 43 74 53 56. Hostel accommodation for 18-25 year olds with jobs or training placements. Advance booking usually necessary.

Union des Maisons d'Etudiants, 93 boulevard St Michel, 75005 Paris. Tel: 46 34 11 16.

Union Nationale des Etudiants Locataires, 120 rue Nôtre Dame de Champs, 75006 Paris. Tel: 46 33 30 78.

## CULTURAL, EDUCATIONAL AND SOCIAL

Alliance Française (the international French cultural institute), 101 boulevard Raspail, 75270 Paris. Tel: 45 44 38 28. UK address: 6 Cromwell Place, London SW7 2JN. Tel: (071) 723 6439. French language classes.

Association for the Study of Modern and Contemporary France, 13 Cantelowes Road, London NW1 9XP. Tel: (071) 267 2402. For French teachers and researchers.

Association France-Grande Bretagne, 17 rue Philibert Delorme, 75017 Paris. Tel: 47 66 43 01. Also 47 bis rue Barberis 06000 Nice. Tel: 93 89 09 55.

British Association of the Alpes-Maritimes, Nice. Tel: 93 88 62 70.

British Council, 9 rue Constantine, 75007 Paris. Tel: 45 55 54 99.

British Institute in Paris, 9 rue Constantine, 75007 Paris. Tel: 45 55 71 91.

Centre Regional des Oeuvres Universitaires et Scolaires (CROUS), 8 rue Jean Calvin, 75005 Paris.

Council of International Educational Exchange, 49 rue Pierre Charron, 75008 Paris. Tel: 43 59 23 69. Can provide a student ID card qualifying for a wide variety of concessions.

English Language Library for the Blind, 5 avenue Daniel Lesueur, 75007 Paris. Tel: 47 34 56 10.

European Council of International Schools, 21(b) Lavant Street, Petersfield, Hampshire GU32 3EL. Tel: (0730) 68244.

Franco-British Society, Room 636, Linen Hall, 162-168 Regent Street, London W1R 5TB. Tel: (071) 734 0815. Exists to encourage British understanding of French artistic, scientific, social and economic achievements, through travel, personal contacts and meetings. Publishes a journal twice a year. Membership includes individuals and firms. Established in 1944.

Franco-Scottish Society, 9 North Park Terrace, Edinburgh EH4 1DP. An old-established (1895) organisation founded to promote Franco-Scottish friendship. It has several local branches.

International Baccalaureate Organisation, 18 Woburn Square, London WC1H 0NS. Tel: (071) 637 1682. Publishes a *General Guide* and *Bulletin*.

Ministère de l'Education Nationale, 110 rue de Grenelle, 75357 Paris. Tel: 45 50 10 10.

Office Nationale des Universités et Ecoles Françaises, 96 boulevard Raspail, 75272 Paris Cedex 06. Tel: 42 22 26 95.

Society for French Studies, Department of French, University of Nottingham, Nottingham NG7 2RD. An organisation of some 1,700 individual members and organisations, it exists to promote French studies in higher education in Britain and the Commonwealth. It publishes a quarterly journal (*French Studies*).

YWCA, 22 rue de Naples, 75008 Paris. Tel: 45 22 72 70.

## BUSINESS CONTACTS

### Business contacts in Britain
DATAR, 21-24 Grosvenor Place, London SW1X 7HU. Tel: (071) 235 5148. The French industrial development agency which produces information on a wide variety of French commercial matters.

Export Credit Guarantee Department (ECGD), Export House, 50 Ludgate Hill, London EC4M 7AY. Tel: (071) 382 7000.

French Embassy (Financial Counsellor). Tel: (071) 235 8080.

Overseas Trade Division, Department of Trade and Industry, 1 Victoria Street, London SW1H 0ET. Tel: (071) 215 7877 (French country desk).

SITPRO, Almack House, 26 King Street, London SW1W 6QW. Tel: (071) 930 0532. The Simplification of International Trade Procedures Board, an independent body set up to help exporters.

## Business contacts in France

British Embassy, 35 rue Faubourg St Honoré, 75008 Paris. The Financial and Commercial Counsellor, Tel: 42 66 91 42. There are branches of the Commercial Section in Bordeaux, Lille, Lyon and Marseille.

Centre Français du Commerce Extériur (French Centre for Foreign Trade), 10 avenue d'Léna, 75016 Paris. Tel: 45 05 30 00.

DATAR, 1 avenue Charles Floquet, 75007 Paris. Tel: 47 83 61 20. The French industrial development agency.

Franco-British Chamber of Commerce and Industry, 8 rue Cimarosa, 75016 Paris. Tel: 45 05 13 08. Publishes a monthly journal *Cross Channel Trade*. The Chamber also has offices in Marseille, Merignac, Lille, Le Havre, Lyon, Rouen, Cherbourg, Strasbourg, and Nice. It is able to provide a wide variety of commercial information, details of trade and professional bodies, contacts, reception and interview facilities (for a fee), and runs a Junior Section for business people aged up to 40.

Ministère de l'Economie et des Finances, Direction des Relations Economiques Extérieures, 41 Quai Branly, 75700 Paris. Tel: 45 55 92 90. For information on international trade.

Ministère de l'Economie et des Finances, Direction Générale des Douanes et Droits Indirects, Division des Autorisations Commerciales (Importations), 8 rue de la Tour Dames, 75009 Paris. Tel: 42 80 67 22. Import and export licences.

Organisation for Economic Cooperation and Development (OECD), Château de la Muette, 2 rue André Pascal, 75775 Paris Cedex 16.

## British banks in France

Barclays Bank SA, 33 rue du Quatre Septembre, 75002 Paris. Tel: 42 65 65 65. Telex: 210015. Also: 6 Rond Point des Champs Elysées, 75008 Paris. Tel: 43 59 15 26. Telex: 650955. 24 Ave Kléber, 75016 Paris. Tel: 45 00 86 86. Telex: 611952.

Grindlays Bank, 7 rue Meyerbeer, 75428 Paris Cedex 09. Tel: 42 66 62 22.

Hong Kong and Shanghai Banking Corporation, 18 rue de la Paix, 750 8 Paris. Tel: 42 61 57 62. Telex: 210321.

International Westminster Bank plc, 18 place Vendôme, 75021 Paris Cedex 01. Tel: 42 60 37 40. Telex: 210393.

Lloyds Bank International (France) plc, 43 boulevard des Capucines, 75061 Paris Cedex 02. Tel: 42 61 51 25 and 42 61 50 63. Telex: 210097 or 680774.

Midland Bank France SA, 6 rue Piccini, 75116 Paris. Tel: 45 02 80 80. Telex: 648022 F MIFRA.

**Miscellaneous**

Bibliothèque Nationale, 58 rue de Richelieu, 75002 Paris. Tel: 47 42 02 51, is one of the most famous libraries in the world. The library is open weekdays from 9h to 18h. Books may never be taken out of the library.

Department of Social Security (Overseas Branch), Newcastle-upon-Tyne, NE98 1YX.

French Publishing Group, 15a Elizabeth Street, London SW1. Tel: (071) 730 3477. Information on French newspapers and magazines and how to advertise in them.

Institute of Linguists, 24a Highbury Grove, London N5 2EA. Tel: (071) 359 7445. Can recommend members who are available for translation work.

Institute of Translation & Interpreting, 318a Finchley Road, London NW3 5HT. Tel: (071) 794 9931.

Libraries: There are free municipal libraries (**biliothèques munici-pales**) in the town halls (**mairies**) of each **arrondissement**. For their addresses, look under **Mairies de Paris** in the telephone directory.

SOS-Help. The Paris-based English language helpline: 47 23 80 80.

# Further Reading

## EXPLORING FRANCE

Cabanne, Pierre, *France*. Translated from the French (Helm, 1988). 416pp, illustrated, with maps.

Cole, Robert. *Traveller's History of France* (Windrush Press, 1988). 178pp, illustrated paperback.

Collins, Martin. *Visitor's Guide to the French Coast* (Moorland Publishing, 1985). 160pp, hardback and paperback editions, illustrated.

Du Vignaud, Bertrand. *The Historic Houses, Castles and Gardens of France*. (Newnes, 1986). 376pp, illustrated paperback. An official guide to sites open to the public.

Hamilton, Ronald. *Holiday History of France* (Hogarth Press, 1985). 256pp, paperback.

Hunter, R & Wickers, D. *Classic Walks in France* (Oxford Illustrated Press, 1985). Illustrated.

James, John. *Traveller's Key to Medieval France* (Harrap Columbus, 1987). 336pp, illustrated paperback.

Pereire, A and Zuylen, G van. *Private Gardens of France* (Weidenfeld & Nicolson, 1983). 224pp, fully illustrated.

Sullivan J and Waite, C. *Villages of France* (Weidenfeld & Nicolson, 1988). 160pp, colour paperback.

Sanger, Andrew. *Exploring Rural France* (Helm, 1990). 208pp, illustrated paperback. Revised edition.

White, Freda. *Three Rivers of France: Dordogne, Lot and Tarn* (Faber, 1984). 232pp, paperback. Reissued by Pavilion Books, 1989, 85 colour illustrations.

Young, Edward. *Shell Guide to France* (Michael Joseph, 1983). 464pp, illustrated paperback.

Waite, Charlie. *Landscape in France* (Elm Tree Books, 1987). 160pp, fully illustrated.

## LIVING IN FRANCE

Brown, Karen. *French Country Inns and Château Hotels* (Harrap Columbus, 1987). 204pp, illustrated paperback.

Dyson, Henry. *French Real Property and Succession Law* (Hale, 1988). 240pp, paperback.

Farndale, W A J. *French Hospitals and Medical Care Services* (Ravenswood, 1975). 72pp.

*France: Economist Business Travellers Guides* (Business Books, 1990). 192pp, illustrated hardback.

*French Country Welcome* (Fédération Nationale des Gîtes Ruraux/ Fivedit, 1990). 456pp, paperback.

Hempshell, Mark. *How to Get a Job in France* (How To Books, 1993). 160pp, paperback.

Holland, Philip. *Living in France* (Hale 1989). 4th edition. 260pp hardback.

Kristen, Clive. *How to Rent & Buy Property in France* (How To Books, 1993). 160pp, paperback.

Mazzawi, Rosalind. *Long Stays in France* (David & Charles, 1990). Hardback.

Price, Kirtsen. *French Country Bed and Breakfasts* (Harrap, 1990). 204pp, illustrated paperback.

Scholey, Andrew. *French Homes for the British* (Wisefile, 1990). 162pp, illustrated paperback.

Warren Laetitia de and Nollet, Catherine. *Setting Up in France* (Merehurst, 1989). 193pp, illustrated.

## FRENCH TRAVEL GUIDES

Altman. France: *Berlitz Blueprint* (Berlitz, 1989). 352pp, illustrated paperback.

Automobile Association. *101 Routes in France* (Automobile Association, 1985). 160pp, illustrated paperback with maps.

Barrett, Frank, Boulton, S, and Gill, C. *France Without Tears* (The Telegraph/Brittany Ferries, 1987). 192pp, illustrated paperback with maps.

*Berlitz Country Guide to France* (Berlitz Guides, 1987). 256pp, paperback, 100 colour illustrations.

Binns, Richard. *France à la Carte* (Corgi, 1986). 143pp, illustrated with maps.

— *French Leave Favourites* (Chiltern House, 1986). 208pp, illustrated.

— *French Leave 3* (Corgi, 1986). 319pp, illustrated paperback. Third edition.

— *Hidden France* (Corgi, 1986). 160pp, illustrated paperback. Revised edition.

— *En Route: The French Autoroute Guide* (Collins, 1986). Illustrated paperback, polyglot edition (English/French/German/Dutch).

Dean, Michael. *France Off the Beaten Track* (Moorland Publishing, 1988). Paperback, 319pp with illustrations and maps.

Fodor. *France 1990* (Fodor's Travel Publications, 1990). 512pp, illustrated paperback.

France. *Michelin Motoring Atlas of France* (Hamlyn 1990), 394pp, paperback.

Hindley, Geoffrey. *Days Out in France* (Columbus, 1988). 192pp, illustrated paperback.

Hoefer, H J (Editor), *France: Insight Guides* (Harrap, 1987). 352pp, fully illustrated in colour.

Kane, Robert S. *France at its Best: Passport Guides* (Columbus, 1986). 440pp, paperback.

Martin, Collette. *A to Z of Holidays in France* (Harrap, 1988). 208pp, illustrated paperback.

Moore, Inge & James. *France at a Glance: A Holiday Handbook for All* (Settle and Bendall, 1984). 200pp, hardback and paperback editions.

Phillips, Harry. *Caravanning Through France* (Navigator Publications, 1987). 320pp, illustrated. Revised edition.

Robertson, Ian. *France: Blue Guide* (A & C Black, 1988). 956pp, illustrated paperback.

Rosenbaum, M. *Mediterranean France: Travellers Guides* (Thornton Cox, 1990). 200pp illustrated paperback.

*Routiers Guide to France* (Ebury Press, 1990). 288pp, illustrated paperback.

Steinbecker, Earl. *40 Daytrips in France* (Hastings House/Columbus, 1986). 256pp, illustrated paperback.

Titchmarsh, Peter & Helen. *Exploring France: A Comprehensive Guide for the Discerning Traveller* (Jarrolds, 1989). 272pp, illustrated paperback.

## FRENCH FOOD AND WINE

Busselle, Michael. *Wine Lover's Guide to France* (Pavilion Books, 1988). 256pp, fully illustrated paperback.

Lynch, K. *Wine Buyer's Tour of France: Adventures on the Wine Route* (Bodley Head, 1989). 286pp.

Millau, Christian. *Dining in France* (Sidgwick & Jackson, 1987). Illustrated paperback. 176pp.

Millon, Marc and Kim. *Wine Roads of France: Complete Companion Guide* (Equation Books, 1989). 416pp, illustrated hardback.

Monahan, P (Editor). *French Hotels and their Restaurants* (William Curtis, 1990). 144pp, illustrated paperback.

Neillands, Robin. *Guide to Wining and Dining in France* (Ashford Books, 1990). 180pp, illustrated.

Philpot, Don. *The Vineyards of France* (Moorland Publishing, 1987). 320pp, hardback and paperback editions.

Price, Pamela Vandyke. *France for the Gourmet Traveller* (Harrap, 1988). 320pp, paperback.

Tordo, Rene. French Menus Interpreted (Navigator Publishing, 1988). 4th edition, 88pp, paperback.

Wells, Patricia. *Food Lover's Guide to France* (Methuen, 1988). 400pp, illustrated paperback.

White, F and Griffin, S W. *French Food and Customs* (Hodder, 1981). Paperback.

*Wines and Winelands of France: Geological Journeys under the Direction of Charles Pomerol* (McCarta, 1989). 369pp.

Youell and Kimball. *Pocket Guide to French Food and Wine* (Xanadu Publications, 1985). 240pp, illustrated paperback.

## FRENCH CULTURE AND SOCIETY

Ardagh, John. *France Today* (Penguin, 1988). 656pp, paperback. Revised edition.

Braudel, Fernand. *The Identity of France*, translation by Sian Reynolds. Vol 1: History and Environment (Collins, 1988). 432pp.

Carre, Jean Jacques. *French Economic Growth*, translated from the French by J P Hatfield (Oxford University Press, 1975). 602pp.

Coveney and Kempa. *Guide to French Institutions* (Nelson, 1984). 72pp, paperback.

Derbyshire, I. *Politics in France: From Giscard to Mitterand* (Chambers, 1990). 224pp, paperback.

Dunlop, Fiona. *Paris Art Guide* (Black, 1988). 164pp, illustrated paperback.

Ellis, D L. *Life in a French Family* (Harrap, 1984). 111pp, illustrated paperback.

Cobban, Alfred. *History of Modern France, Vol 3: 1871-1962* (Penguin, 1990). 272pp, paperback.

Hanley, David. *Contemporary France: Politics and Society since 1945* (Routledge & Kegan Paul, 1984). 372pp, illustrated.

Hantrais, Linda. *Contemporary French Society* (Macmillan, 1982). 224pp, illustrated paperback.

Holmes G and Fawcett P D. *Contemporary French Economy* (Macmillan, 1983). Paperback.

Manston, Peter. *Antique Fairs of France: Travel Keys Series* (Batsford, 1989). 206pp, paperback. Illustrated.

Mazey, S and Newman, M. *Mitterand's France* (Croom Helm, 1987). 256pp, illustrated.

Mehling, F N. *France: A Cultural Guide* (Phaidon, 1985). 800pp, with 750 colour illustrations.

Paul, Elliott. *Narrow Street* (Harrap, 1986). A picture of Paris social life originally published by Cresset in 1942. 230pp, paperback.

Porter, Melinda Chamber. *Reflections on Contemporary French Art and Culture* (Oxford University Press, 1987). 256pp, illustrated.

Reid, Joyce (editor). *Concise Oxford Dictionary of French Literature* (Oxford University Press, 1976). 676pp, hardback and paperback editions.

Ramball, Paul. *French Blues: A Not-so Sentimental Journey through Lives and Memories in Modern France* (Heinemann, 1989). 225pp.

Ross G and Hoffman, S (Editors). *The Mitterand Experiment: Continuity and Change in Modern France* (Polity, 1987). 363pp, paperback.

Slater, Malcolm. *Contemporary French Politics* (Macmillan, 1985). 275pp, paperback.

Slesin, Suzanne. *French Style* (Thames & Hudson, 1982). 288pp. Interior design and similar subjects, with 450 colour illustrations.

Smith, Bradley. *France: A History of Art* (Weidenfeld & Nicolson, 1984). 296pp, fully illustrated in colour.

Zeldin, Theodore. *The French* (Collins, 1983). 512pp, paperback. A leading study.

## BUSINESS

*ABECOR Country Reports: France*, Barclays Bank group, Economic Intelligence Unit, 54 Lombard Street, London EC3P 3AH.

*British Business*, weekly news bulletin published by the Department of Trade and Industry, available from HMSO Publications, PO Box 569, London SE1 9NH. Tel: (071) 928 6777, extension 472. Includes details of export markets, trade fairs and exhibitions, customs and tariffs, investment, statistics and similar matters.

*Business Guide to France: World of Information* (Longman, 1986). 61pp.

*Country Profiles: France*, published by the British Overseas Trade Broad and regularly updated. Covers the regions of France, industry, trade and the economy, opportunities for British exporters, design and technical considerations, marketing, travel, work and residence in France, investment, export conditions and other information. Exports to Europe Branch, Department of Trade and Industry, 1 Victoria Street, London SW1H 0ET. Tel: (071) 215 5303.

*Cross Channel Trade*, magazine published by the Franco-British Chamber of Commerce and Industry, 8 rue Cimarosa, 75116 Paris. Tel: 45 05 13 08. News, articles and features of interest to the Anglo-French business community.

*Doing Business In France*. Publication issued by the Franco-British Chamber of Commerce (see *Cross Channel Trade* above).

*Economic Report: France*, Lloyds Bank Group Economics Department, 71 Lombard Street, London EC3P 3BS.

*European Business*. Published quarterly by SEED (Société européenne d'édition et de diffusion), 28 boulevard Raspail, 75007 Paris. International management organisation devoted to exerting educational leadership in Europe's business community, fostering links between managers, companies, and business and research centres in Europe.

*Hints to Exporters: France*. A useful pocket-sized booklet available from The Department of Trade and Industry (Hints to Exporters Unit), Lime Grove, Eastcote, Ruislip, Middlesex HA4 8SG. Tel: (081) 866 8771, extension 255 (or any Regional DTI office).

*Mail Order Houses in France*, Department of Trade and Industry. (See *Country Profiles: France* above.)

*Marketing Consumer Goods in France*, Department of Trade and Industry, as above.

*OECD Economic Surveys: France*. Available from HMSO, See *Hints to Exporters: France*

*Spotlight France*, Midland Bank International, 110 Cannon Street, London EC4N 6AA.

*Taxation in France*, Parkinson Publishing, 1990. 176pp, paperback.

### Reference materials

*Annuaires des Participations Etrangères*, 46 rue de Rome, Paris. Participation of foreign firms in companies established in France.

*Bottin Europe, Bottin International, Bottin Professions, Bottin Departments*. Business registers, with indexes in English. Published by the Society Didot, 28 rue du Dr Finlay, 75015 Paris.

*Les Cahiers de l'Institut d'Aménagement et d'Urbanisme de la région d'Ile de France*, 21-23 rue Miollis, 75732 Paris Cedex 15. A bilingual periodical with notes on industrial development and urbanism in the Paris area. Very useful for heads of enterprises. Gives profiles of enterprises, human resources, transportation, marketing, planning, and urbanization of new industrial and residential areas; also deals with energy, landscape, etc.

*Kompass France*, 22 avenue Franklin D. Roosevelt, 75008 Paris. A three-volume, comprehensive industrial directory giving company data for most firms in France.

*Monde Economique*. Annual economic review published by the French Newspaper, *Le Monde*, 7 rue des Italiens, 75427 Paris Cedex 09.

# Index

# Other books in this series

**How to Get a Job Abroad**
Roger Jones

This top-selling title is essential for everyone planning to spend a period abroad. It contains a big reference section of medium and long-term job opportunities and possibilities, arranged by region and country of the world, and by profession/occupation. There are more than 130 pages of specific contacts and leads, giving literally hundreds of addresses and much hard-to-find information. There is a classified guide to overseas recruitment agencies, and even a multi-lingual guide to writing application letters. 'A fine book for anyone considering even a temporary overseas job.' *The Evening Star*. 'A highly informative and well researched book. . . containing lots of hard information and a first class reference section. . . A superb buy.' *The Escape Committee Newsletter*. 'A valuable addition to any careers library.' *Phoenix (Association of Graduate Careers Advisory Services)*. 'An excellent addition to any careers library . . . Compact and realistic. . . There is a wide range of reference addresses covering employment agencies, specialist newspapers, a comprehensive booklist and helpful addresses . . . All readers, whether careers officers, young adults or more mature adults, will find use for this book.' *Newscheck/Careers Services Bulletin*.

288pp illus. 1 85703 003 6. Second Edition

**How to Get a Job in Europe**
Mark Hempshell

The Single European Market and Europe's rise as the world's leading economic unit, has made it the place to get a job. This new **How To** book is the first to set out exactly what opportunities exist in Europe. It contains step-by-step guidance on how to find the vacancies, how to apply, and how to understand and adapt to the cultural and legal framework. Packed throughout with key contacts, sample documents and much hard-to-find information, this book will be an absolutely essential starting point for everyone job-hunting in Europe, whether as a school or college leaver, graduate trainee, technician or professional — and indeed anyone wanting to live and work as a European whether for just a summer vacation or on a more permanent basis. Mark Hempshell is a freelance writer who specialises in writing on overseas employment.

160pp illus. 1 85703 060 5.

**How to Get a Job in France**
Mark Hempshell

This is the first book which sets out clearly how to get a job in France, whether for example in catering, tourism, teaching, computing, retailing, or other craft, industry, business or profession. We are all today not only part of a national economy, but a European — and even global — marketplace; and for those wiling to surmount cultural and language barriers, the rewards in standard and quality of life can be considerable. This most informative book is packed with helpful information and guidance on every aspect of the French employment scene and will be a valuable resource for everyone concerned with the growing subject of international employment. Mark Hempshell is a specialist researcher and author on the European employment scene.

159pp illus. 1 85703 081. 8.

**How to Live & Work in Belgium**
Marvina Shilling

Researched and written by a specialist on Belgian affairs, this is a complete manual of essential information on Belgium from entering the country to taking up residence, coping with the language, living in Brussels, Antwerp and other major cities, understanding the business, official and legal environment, the cost of living and other vital facts and advice for executives, officials, technicians, students, teachers and others. 'Interesting, easy to read and full of fascinating information . . . Gives a succinct and enlightening explanation for the use of both the French and Dutch language and the political tensions engendered by this language split.' *Phoenix/Association of Graduate Careers Advisory Services.* 'A crisp and clear resumé. . . If companion volumes are on a similar par, a European collection would be particularly appropriate.' *Newscheck/ Careers Service Bulletin.*

139pp illus. 1 85703 053 2.

## How to Live & Work in Germany
Nessa Loewenthal

West and East Germany formally became a single nation in October 1990. The real work of unification is likely to take many years, but this process — added to the ultimate potential for economic and cultural growth — makes this an exciting time to live in Germany. Whether you are planning to relocate for three months or three years, this is the book for you. It covers such practical topics as entry requirements, transportation, money matters, housing, schools, insurance and much besides. It also includes valuable pointers to German values, customs, business practices and etiquette to help you make the most of your stay. Nessa Loewenthal is Director of Trans Cultural Services, and a consultant specialising in intercultural briefing. 'Detailed help is given on how to find work in Germany including . . . a comprehensive list of organisations which offer the chance to combine the experience of living in Germany with a useful activity.' *Phoenix/Association of Graduate Careers Advisory Services.*

142pp illus. 1 85703 006 0.

## How to Live & Work in Italy
Amanda Hinton

Another new addition to the 'How to Live & Work in' range, written by an experienced travel author and English resident in Italy. Essential pointers to obtaining Italian-style accommodation, employment, business life, recreation, money matters and a great deal more — packed with essential reference information.

160pp illus. 1 85703 034 6.

## How to Live & Work in Portugal
Sue Tyson-Ward

A new guide for short and longstay visitors to one of Europe's oldest, most charming and best-value countries: covers entry requirements, finding a place to stay, employment, doing business, getting around, health, education and more.

160pp illus. 1 85703 085 0.

**How to Live & Work in Spain**
Robert A C Richards

Long popular with Britons for holidays and retirement, Spain is now an
increasingly important focus for commercial life. Written by a British
expatriate who has lived and worked in Spain for more than 25 years,
this new book provides a use-friendly guide for everyone planning to live
in Spain on a temporary or permanent basis, whether for business,
professional purposes, study, leisure or retirement. Written with
considerable gusto, the book gives a fascinating warts'n'all account of
Spain's variegated lifestyles and how to cope. 'As well as the sort of
information one might expect eg work permits, visas, property buying
and financial matters, there is so much additional information on health
care, travel, holidays, history, geography etc that I feel it would be a good
read for the more casual visitor. . . The information is presented in an
orderly and interesting way' *Phoenix/Association of Graduate Careers
Advisory Services.*

160pp illus. 1 85703 011 7.

**How to Rent & Buy a Property in France**
Clive Kristen

Interest in French property has never been greater. Prices are lower than
in the UK, and the French climate and culture are powerful incentives to
renters and buyers. Honest independent advice, however, is hard to come
by. If you are thinking about buying or renting a second home, or
moving to France to work or retire, this practical book will guide you
step-by-step through the pitfalls of loans, contracts, and even setting up a
profitable gîte business. It covers: your renting/buying decision, the
options, regions, rentals and timeshares, relocating to France, banking,
taxation, wills, mortgages, loans, insurance, the purchase process,
building or buying a property under construction, running your own gîte
business, and more. Complete with specimen forms and documents. Clive
Kristen MEd is an experienced teacher and lecturer with a special interest
in France and the French legal system, and has full personal experience
of buying and renting property in France.

160pp illus. 1 85703 072 9.